OTTOMAN EGYPT

AND THE EMERGENCE OF THE MODERN WORLD 1500–1800

OTTOMAN EGYPT

AND THE EMERGENCE OF THE MODERN WORLD 1500–1800

NELLY HANNA

The American University in Cairo Press
Cairo New York

This edition published in 2014 by
The American University in Cairo Press
113 Sharia Kasr el Aini, Cairo, Egypt
420 Fifth Avenue, New York, NY 10018
www.aucpress.com

Exclusive distribution outside Egypt and North America by I.B.Tauris & Co Ltd., 6 Salem Road, London, W2 4BU

Dar el Kutub No. 23470/13
ISBN 978 977 416 664 8

Dar el Kutub Cataloging-in-Publication Data

Hanna, Nelly
Ottoman Egypt and the Emergence of the Modern World: 1500–1800 / Nelly Hanna.—Cairo: The American University in Cairo Press, 2014
p. cm.
ISBN: 978 977 416 664 8
1. Egypt—History
640—1882
962.03

1 2 3 4 5 18 17 16 15 14

Designed by Jon W. Stoy
Printed in Egypt

Contents

Acknowledgments

My thanks are due to a number of persons and institutions who have helped me to bring this project to fruition. First on this list are the Center for Middle Eastern Studies at Harvard University and Professor Baber Johansen, former director of the Center. He extended an invitation to give the Hamilton Gibb Lectures in October–November 2012. Subsequently, William Granara, present director of the Center, gave further encouragement to the publication of the lectures in book form, and to him I express my deep gratitude.

The lectures were considerably reworked and lengthened, and an introduction was added to make the various articles conform to a set of themes that run across the book. This has entailed extensive research and much rethinking on the way the topics of the lectures were presented. This process required adaptation and extension of the original lectures. Substantial changes were made in the lectures. The chapters in the present book are the outcome of this work. The introduction explains the themes that run throughout the book and elaborates on the way they were applied to the topics covered in the three following chapters.

My gratitude also goes to Peter Gran for helpful suggestions on the text and to Madiha Doss for her comments on early drafts of chapter 2; and to Daniel Woodward, graduate student in the Department of Arab and Islamic Civilizations, who helped me put the manuscript together, made helpful comments, and spared no effort in the many technicalities that this process involved.

1 Egypt from 1600 to 1800: Between Local and Global

The Multiple Narratives of Modern World History

The mainstream textbooks about modern world history have for a long time described the three centuries from 1500 to 1800 as a dynamic period that was the basis for the emergence of the modern world. Their narratives focus on some of the important scientific, cultural, and cconomic developments that took place during these centuries. Among these the most important were the Renaissance and the Reformation, which ushered in scientific and intellectual inquiry; the technological advances that opened the way for the Industrial Revolution; the Scientific Revolution, which was brought about by the discoveries by great thinkers like Copernicus (d. 1543), who questioned the earth as center of the universe, Galileo (d. 1642) and his telescope, Bacon (d. 1626; sometimes called the father of empiricism), Newton (d. 1727; a key figure in the scientific revolution), and William Harvey (d. 1647; the English physician famous for his discoveries about blood circulation). The diffusion of ideas was greatly facilitated by the invention and the spread of the printing press. Moreover, the creation of trading companies, such as the East India Company and the Dutch East India Company, eventually led to colonial domination of large parts of the world. The period was consequently portrayed as the prelude to European world hegemony, which had its sources in the great discoveries and in European expansion into the New

World. Many of these developments were made possible by emerging centralized states, which supported the trading companies and encouraged intellectual and scientific discoveries. In different parts of Europe, powerful states emerged, like that of Philip II of Spain (d. 1598), Peter the Great in Russia (d. 1725), and Louis XIV in France (d. 1715), with strong rulers, often supported by strong military powers. To a considerable extent, the focus tended to privilege elites, whether thinkers who had an impact on intellectual life or the princes and rulers at the head of these growing states.[1]

This narrative of the emergence of the modern world was the standard way of understanding the period from 1500 to 1800. Its explanation was, to a large extent, European oriented. In fact, its analysis leaves out most of the world beyond Europe. This view on the centrality of Europe is clearly articulated by the British historian Hugh Trevor-Roper who, some forty or so years ago, wrote, "The history of the world, for the past five centuries, insofar as it has any significance, has been European history. I do not think that we need to make any apology if our study of history is European-centric."[2]

The non-European world was considered to be more or less outside of history, in a state of limbo or stagnation, until the moment that it came into contact with the west. A recent book by Toby Huff, a scholar whose work has been translated into many languages, reflects a similar view, indicating that this approach continues to have considerable weight in academic circles.[3] In many studies, it still represents the dominant view.

Many of these views can be attributed to nineteenth-century thought. Writers with different intellectual leanings seem to have been in agreement with each other when it came to understanding the non-European world. Marx, writing in the mid-nineteenth century, saw China as a "giant empire . . . vegetating in the teeth of time, insulated by the forced exclusion of general intercourse and thus continuing to dupe itself with delusion of Celestial perfection."[4] His opinion bears a lot of similarity to the Hegelian view, which considered many parts of the non-European world, such as India, Africa, Siberia, and so on, to be 'outside history.' That these views have persisted up to the twenty-first century could in part be due to the intellectual weight of these thinkers.

Prior to the nineteenth century, the histories of the 'other' regions of the world were histories of decline. When great civilizations are mentioned in surveys of the modern or the early modern world—the Chinese, Islamic, or Indian civilizations—they are usually not integrated as active agents or partners, but rather as regions in decline. Thus, these non-European regions only entered history at the moment that they started to follow the European model. This meant that entering world history was equivalent to becoming western. In other words, the history of the emergence of the modern world is a history of the west, and of the way that other peoples learned from or imitated Europeans.

Implicit in these works was a diffusionist approach, which perceived culture as having one center (Europe) from where it was diffused to other regions of the world, with variable degrees of success. This approach was consolidated with the development of imperialism—especially in the form it took in the nineteenth century. It was then projected backward two or three centuries, as a way of understanding the Ottoman Empire or Mughal India. Clearly, alternative approaches need to be developed.

Consequently, the history of many formerly colonized countries was, until a few decades ago, written to make them appcar to have reached the depth of decline just before the period of colonialism or European penetration. For a long time, the historiography of Egypt and the rest of the Ottoman Empire emphasized the negative aspects of the period. In many such studies, the focus was on the despotic nature of rule and the conditions of decay, disorder, or disintegration of society and economy, of culture and learning. The three centuries preceding the French Expedition of 1798 were for a long time portrayed as one of the lowest points of the history of Egypt. The despotic sultanic or state power as the main mover in history left little or no space for society, and as a result the historical development was habitually portrayed as a top-down process. In other studies, the focus was on the inability of the region to keep up with the numerous developments taking place in Europe at the time, such as the Renaissance and the Enlightenment. As a result, while Europe experienced cultural and political progress, the region did not undergo these same developments and sank into decay. It was difficult to try to find a place for Egypt in relation to the regional and world transformations taking place at the time. The decline paradigm negated the possibility of an active role in world history.

The broad lines of this approach to the history of Egypt were similar to the historiography of most other formerly colonized countries. The histories of India and of Persia, for instance, which were written at the start of the twentieth century by colonial administrators like Henry Dodwell (d. 1946), or by military persons like Percy Sykes, also a diplomat and scholar (d. 1945), emphasized all that was negative before the coming of Europeans and showed the positive sides of colonial government. They had in common, whether they were referring to the Ottoman Empire, India, Persia, Southeast Asia, or China, a similar line of thought and a common vocabulary, with often repeated terms like 'backwardness,' 'stagnation,' and 'decline' in relation to Europe, which was always the point of comparison. Eighteenth-century India was, for example, described as a place of chaos and anarchy.

Colonial government was portrayed as an enlightened government with solid achievements in medicine and education, among other fields, bringing modernity to 'backward' countries. The very justification of colonial domination was its civilizing mission; it brought enlightenment and education to so-called primitive societies, such as those in Africa, and to 'backward' societies, like Egypt or Mesopotamia, which were known as great civilizations in the past but which had long since fallen into decline. Colonialism helped them to move these societies from tyranny to enlightenment and the rule of law.[5]

The historical writings that emphasized the weaknesses of these non-European countries during the period from 1500 to 1800 tended to posit a break in continuity between this period and the following one, the nineteenth century and the beginning of the modern period. The moment of European penetration formed the dividing line between the traditional, or static, condition of a society and economy and the entrance into a modern world. Implicit in these views was an emphasis on the incapacities of these regions to modernize or to confront the changes that the modern world brought; traditional societies were incapable of innovation; they were isolated from the developments taking place in the world and consequently could not benefit from new ideas and technologies or contribute to them. There was also a denial that these regions could either construct their own modernity or even contribute to its construction; the possibility that they might have a role in constructing the modern world was not considered. Consequently, modern world history was shown as being created entirely in and by Europe. From there it was diffused to the regions where Europeans had an influence.

To a large extent, these histories failed to show the historical realities of the countries on which they were focused. There was hardly anything written about society, about the way that people ran their lives, or about economies or the way people earned their living. Rather, they reflected the approaches of the nineteenth-century hegemonic or colonial powers toward the countries that they had penetrated or colonized. Such histories were in keeping with the discourse of power that accompanied such penetration or colonialism. This can explain the similarity of the descriptions, sometimes even of the vocabulary, that were applied from areas as diverse as India, Persia, and the Ottoman Empire. These narratives did not consider the possibility that these three great empires, with their diverse populations, their enormous productive activities, and their intensive trade that extended across many parts of the world, might have a transformative role from 1500 to 1800. The absence of great scientists or intellectuals and of men whose names were well known or who had undertaken acts of some notability tended to emphasize the picture of decline.

The emphasis on Europeans as givers and non-European as recipients distorts a much more convoluted, and lesser known, reality. What was perceived as being specifically European and modern was in fact far more complex. In the nineteenth century, once the Industrial Revolution was well under way and colonial powers dominated much of the Third World, numerous inventions and technical innovations initiated in Europe were transferred to regions outside this continent, for instance, in the field of communications, steamships, railways, and telegraphs; in the field of science and technology; and in the field of medicine. The importance of these transfers was considerable and transformative. Nevertheless, to project this backward to the early modern period distorts the realities of the time.

This narrative remained dominant until recent revisionist scholarship proposed an entirely different picture that showed, on the contrary, a period of great dynamism outside Europe, during which there was a significant expansion in both trade and production, as well as growth in the use of money.[6]

Alternatives to Eurocentric Approaches to Modern World History

At present, these ideas are being seriously reconsidered by a number of historians, and their work is changing the way we think of the period as a whole. As a result, these older paradigms are gradually being rehabilitated. Recent studies on Ottoman Egypt, for instance, including my own work, are showing a different picture from that of a despotic sultan, a corrupt Mamluk ruling class, and a society in a state of apathy. Rather, they portray a dynamic society, which was creative, functioned well with its ups and downs, and made sense to those that lived in it. We now have an important body of scholarship on Egypt in the period between the sixteenth and eighteenth centuries, written in Arabic, English, and French, by European scholars such as André Raymond on merchants and artisans; Nicolas Michel on peasants and rural conditions; Michel Tuscherer on the Red Sea trade; and Egyptian scholars like Magdi Guirguis on Copts; Husam Abdul-Mu'ti on textiles, trade, and production; Nasir Ibrahim on relations between Mamluks during the French expedition; and others. This body of scholarship has moved away from the state-oriented writings of an earlier period, and show a different picture of rural and urban economy and society. What we see is a vibrant society and a working economy. Globally, these studies have changed the way we look at the Ottoman period, arguing against the earlier Orientalist views and challenging their basic precepts.

On a broader level, scholars of world history have made important contributions to this debate. They have tried to write histories that integrate nonwestern perspectives, thus enriching and deepening the study of the modern world. Their work can help us to understand local histories (i.e., the history of Egypt) in a different perspective. One line of argument has been to identify some of the broad features and to describe this period of change that touched many parts of the world without being necessarily initiated by any one entity. Such works have focused on the global sea passages that linked the various parts of the world, on the emergence of a world market, and on the creation of large political entities.[7]

Another related line of argument upheld by a number of scholars has been to question the idea that the modern world was created only by Europe. This important body of literature has proposed alternative ways to write modern world history than those histories that viewed Europe and the west as the center of development, enlightenment, and capitalism. Many studies regarding India, Asia, China, and Southeast Asia have successfully questioned these histories, which had dominated scholarship about non-European regions for a long time, portraying Europe as the norm. This literature rejected the models of these non-European regions as places without history, as autonomous in the sense of being impervious to changes going on around them, as being stagnant and in decline, and as awakening only with the emergence of colonialism, when they became the recipients of European culture and technology. This historiography challenged the idea that the experience of the west was the standard for others to follow; it also challenged the idea that Europe, in extending its hegemony, could be considered the core for the transmission of knowledge to the rest of the world.

These studies have initiated different approaches to the subject, both theoretical and empirical. Theorists like Peter Gran argued against these Eurocentric views by showing that European societies were not essentially different from any other societies. Comparisons could be made between European and non-European societies by studying the various paths by which different sets of countries entered the modern world—that, in other words, they reached the twentieth or the twenty-first centuries by channels other than those followed by Europe.[8] Challenges to Eurocentric views of the world also came from other theoretical thinkers such as Samir Amin. He also rejected the idea of a dynamic Europe and stagnant east, considering that capitalism could not be regarded as a uniquely European phenomenon since India, China, the Islamic East, and the Mediterranean all had forms of protocapitalism and had the potential to develop into capitalism. Capitalism was, in other words, a worldwide phenomenon. As it developed into an advanced core and a backward periphery, he considered that regions outside Europe were not in a lesser stage of development toward modernity, but rather they were part of this modernity, albeit a modernity that was different from that in Europe, since the emergence of capitalism created growing inequalities between core and periphery.[9] Scholars like J.M. Blaut have argued against diffusionism, rejecting the idea that there was a single culture, that this culture was formed in Europe, and that it was subsequently diffused to other parts of the world.[10] Historians have convincingly demonstrated that neither India nor Southeast Asia were obscure zones during this time of transformation, but that on the contrary, their trade played a major role in the world economy. The claim that the non-European world was the recipient of this culture but did not contribute to its formation had now definitely been put into question.

New methodologies were developed which gave weight to often neglected parts of the world and integrated them into the major transformations that took place between the fifteenth and eighteenth centuries. Works such as Eric Wolf's *Europe and the People without History*, Jack Goody's *The Theft of History*, or André Gunder Frank's *ReOrient: Global Economy in the Asian Age* are part of a growing literature that, in different ways, tries to integrate into world history the peoples and civilizations that are often left out of the historical narrative, whether natives of America or other non-European civilizations, such as the various civilizations in India, China, and Japan, and to identify 'core' regions outside those in Europe.[11]

These works were further consolidated by arguments from scholars who did not agree that modernity distinguished Europe from other traditional societies and that only Europe had the appropriate universal qualities that could be spread worldwide.[12] Others argued that many of the features of modern world history had their origins outside Europe, and to understand modern world history, these origins have to be included in the picture. Christopher Bayly, for instance, found that competition from Indian textiles worldwide was one of the main triggers of the British Industrial Revolution, a view that basically challenges the way this revolution has long been understood.[13] Another challenge to this narrative came from Eric Williams, the late prime minister of Trinidad and Tobago and one of the earliest writers on this subject. Like Bayly,

Williams questioned the idea that the Industrial Revolution was a purely British phenomenon, arguing that in the seventeenth century, Caribbean sugar production not only funded British industrialization but also contributed to the development of modern methods of industrial production. The large number of workers in one place, the strict labor discipline, the division of labor into work units, all these were elements that had their origin in the sugar plantations of the Caribbean, not in Manchester, and they were later implemented in industrial practices.[14] Williams's work shows the impact that the periphery had on the core, by indicating how the Caribbean experience was a predecessor of the British Industrial Revolution. Such revisionist views have contributed to changing some of the basic precepts of the traditional narrative.

As a result of these initiatives, the historiography of some regions of formerly colonized countries has taken huge steps forward, and the way that their histories are now written has changed radically.

The worldwide concern to counteract Eurocentrism by proposing alternative ways of writing history has nevertheless left out many regions. So far, there has been little mention of Egypt, Arab lands, or the Ottoman Empire in many historical works dealing with the subject. In spite of the work of scholars like Suraiya Faroqhi and Daniel Goffman, who have written important studies that show the close and complex relationships between the Ottoman Empire and Europe, or Giancarlo Casale's recent book on the participation of the Ottomans in the Age of Exploration, which shows the common traits between European explorations and Ottoman ones, we still have some way to go before this region is seriously considered part of the world historical developments of the period.[15] It is now time to find out where these regions stand in relation to the developments in the field. This interest may now be reaching Arabic studies and overcoming a bit of the Orientalist legacy that dominated the field for a long time. What other non-western fields of studies achieved a decade or more ago is now becoming possible in the case of Egypt.

The reconsideration of the traditional thesis is to a large extent based on the assumption that the formation of modern world history was part of a complex process, and that our world today is a much too complex entity for it to be attributed to one single region (Europe) or to be the achievement of a handful of great men. This means that we need to "decentralize world history" and see it as developing in a process of many parts rather than as a history of Europe and of its imperial projects, or, in the words of Christopher Bayly, to understand the multiple and interconnected origins of global change. He and others have argued that early modern globalization was multicentered, and that the 'expansion of Europe' was but one of several examples of globalization. Even in the later period, when European nations extended their hegemonies over large parts of the world, not all significant change was initiated by them and beneath the surface the world continued to be multicentered.[16]

Rather than projecting nineteenth-century ideologies backward, one can try to see non-European regions in their own context. Bringing into the picture as important a region as the Ottoman Empire in general, or Egypt in particular, can help to achieve a more balanced picture of how developments from 1500 to 1800 had an impact on those of the subsequent period. We need to rethink much of what was written about this region and about its relationship to a broader regional and world context.

Egypt in the Light of World Transformations, 1500–1800

The chapters in this volume address Egypt's role in relation to the transformations from 1500 to 1800 and in the developments that took place subsequently in the nineteenth century. These chapters also suggest that Egypt contributed to the formation of the modern world, challenging the idea that this country was outside of world history before 1800, an autonomous entity, unaffected by larger social forces until it was introduced to European modernity. The book analyzes some of those spheres where there were links between developments taking place in Egypt and the broader changes of the period. One can thus also connect local conditions to world conditions.

We must move between a focus on specific and concrete conditions experienced in Egypt and a broader and more general focus on world transformations. Often, because of its very nature, world history has tended to focus on the macro level. This book has as its starting point the micro level of local conditions and from there moves to the macro level of world conditions. Whenever possible, it does so by writing a kind of 'world history from below' that shows how society, often how certain people, usually anonymous, responded to these conditions, were affected by them, and perhaps even contributed to shaping them.

One way to re-think these issues is to view them in the light of the major trends from 1500 to 1800, notably that this was a period of great commercial expansion, and to define Egypt's place in the changes. Many parts of the world from 1500 to 1800 underwent significant transformations. One reason was the growth in world trade. This was a consequence of the world maritime routes, which linked distant parts of the world to each other on a regular basis. The volume of merchandise underwent considerable expansion. Markets grew, and more consumer goods were produced. Broader regions, which were often far apart, became included in the trade circuits as, for the first time, America became part of these circuits. It was consequently a period of extensive exchanges at many levels, not only commercial, but also cultural. Technologies were exchanged, fashions moved from one region to another, and so on.

But Egypt's place in world history of the period and its impact on subsequent developments is a subject that still lags behind. For a long time, scholars argued that after the fifteenth-century circumnavigation of the Cape of Good Hope by the Portuguese and their settlement in India, Egypt's Red Sea transit trade, which was at the heart of its economy, had declined as a result of the Portuguese channeling the pepper trade through the newly discovered route directly to Europe. Thanks to the work of André Raymond, we now know that the coffee trade became a major item of the Red Sea trade, largely replacing the spice trade of the earlier period.[17] Even though few will now uphold this view, it was replaced by equally negative views.

Among the other proposals that have been put forward to explain Egypt's commercial position during this period is that, in a general way, the southern Mediterranean region was in decline from the sixteenth century onward. The basis of this argument is that it suffered as a result of the considerable economic development of northern European powers, such as the Dutch in the seventeenth century, leading to a change as the center of gravity moved from Venice in the south to Amsterdam in the north. Moreover, the expansion of European powers toward North and South America resulted in the development of a very active Atlantic trade. The Mediterranean began receding in world importance from that point.[18] This view oversimplifies the situation, leaving out important developments of the seventeenth and eighteenth centuries. In reality, the Ottoman, Safavid, and Mughal empires, in the centuries prior to colonialism, had active commercial relations, both with each other and with other parts of the world. However, these three huge empires were usually left out of the historiographic picture.

Another perception of where the southern Mediterranean stood in relation to world history from 1500 to 1800 was the core periphery model, elaborated by Immanuel Wallerstein.[19] However, it is now generally accepted that this model of a European core region and a periphery for the non-European world is not applicable to the Ottoman Empire from 1500 to 1800. The Ottoman Empire in general did not become peripheral before the nineteenth century. As far as Egypt was concerned, no European power had hegemony in this region; nor was Europe yet the industrial power that emerged in the nineteenth century, searching for cheap raw materials and markets for its finished goods; nor, finally, was it the center from which flowed science, knowledge, technology, and fashion. Nevertheless, even though this model has been generally rejected, it has not yet been replaced. It would be wrong to conclude that the countries where European hegemony had not reached were impervious to these changes that were affecting so many other parts of the world. Therefore the subject at hand is the historical conditions before European hegemony.

Two matters were relevant in shaping the relationship of the Ottoman Empire to modern world history. The first is trade. Evidence shows that Egypt was affected by the worldwide expansion of trade in more ways than one. Although from a much earlier date, Egypt was deeply involved in international trade, playing a vital role in the exchanges between east and west, the sixteenth century nevertheless brought about significant changes. During the sixteenth century, Egypt's incorporation into the Ottoman Empire encouraged closer trading relations with commercial centers in the eastern Mediterranean, especially with Istanbul. Egypt's commercial activity was, at about that time, supplemented by an expanding trade in coffee, which became a worldwide commodity controlled mainly by merchants in Cairo. The enormous amounts of coffee they handled were destined for many parts of the Ottoman Empire and Europe. Coffee tended to replace spices as the most lucrative merchandise these merchants handled. André Raymond's work on the eighteenth-century trade in coffee, spices, and Indian textiles has shed light on the importance of this economic sector and on the profits it provided.

Moreover, there was an expansion of trade circuits affecting the Ottoman Empire as a whole, Egypt included. These various circuits became linked to the broader trading circuits that linked to the Indian Ocean and the Atlantic Ocean. The study by Mehmet Bulut has shown the connections that were being formed between the Ottoman Empire and the Atlantic trade in the seventeenth century.[20] Also in the seventeenth century, Europe and America were introduced to the coffee coming from Yemen across the Red Sea through Egypt, and soon coffeehouses flourished in many European cities. The Ottoman world was introduced to the tobacco coming from America. Both commodities gained enormous popularity and were widely consumed. The gold and silver that were extracted from Central and South American mines entered the circuit of trade between Europe, the Ottoman Empire, and Asia. And as one of the chapters in this book shows, the cloth made in Egypt was sent to clothe the slaves in the Caribbean. The shift to bulk rather than to luxury merchandise was itself indicative of an expansion in trading. All this shows that the traditional trading circuits were broadened and trading became more intensive, facilitated by new maritime routes as well as by a rise in consumption.

The second feature that characterized the region's commercial position is that prior to the nineteenth century, no single power dominated the region. There were several strong empires, both in the Islamic world (Mughal, Safavid, and Ottoman) and in the western world (Spanish, Hapsburg, British, and Russian), none of which was able to impose its hegemony on the regions of the Middle East. There were multiple centers of power, making it difficult for any one European state to dominate, or to allow any of them to emerge as a hegemonic power.[21] By contrast, colonial domination by Europeans was easier and more rapid in regions that had weak or unstable political entities, as in the Americas, which in the sixteenth century experienced the hegemony of European powers. The distorted portrayal of 'the west and the rest' does not make this distinction between the conditions in America where, in the sixteenth century, as a result of the great discoveries, European powers were able to control large territories, and the Mediterranean, where this did not happen, to a great extent because of these large empires. Under colonial conditions of the nineteenth century, exchanges tended much more to be undertaken between colonizer and colonized; in this way, colonizer powers could control much of the trading activity of the colonized region. British–Egyptian trade of the late nineteenth century is a good example of this dual type of relation. Roger Owen, in his study of the cotton economy of Egypt, has shown how, as the British came to dominate the politics and economy of Egypt, trading relations followed the same path, and Britain's trade with Egypt came to exclude other trading partners. Exchanges with Britain stood at about a tenth of Egypt's trade at the beginning of the nineteenth century, increasing to about half by the middle of the century, while at the same time, more of Egypt's cotton produce was destined to be sent to Britain, where it was needed for British manufactures.[22]

The situation prior to 1800 was somewhat different, and these trading activities were much more diverse. Commercial as well as other exchanges took place with numerous partners and in various directions. One could consider this one of the distinctive features of this period, as far as the Ottoman Empire, Egypt included, was concerned; this was a period during which the expansion of world commerce coincided with the fact that exchanges were not dominated by a single partner but were undertaken with multiple partners in different directions.

The conditions from 1600 to 1800 can be illustrated by showing the diversity and dynamism of the exchanges between the Ottoman, Safavid, and Mughal empires. Clearly there were important trading relations.[23] Given the state of present scholarship, there is nevertheless much to explore. In all likelihood, the trade between the Mughal and Ottoman empires was of greater importance than Ottoman trade with Europe. One of the agents of the East India Company said in 1690 that the amount of

Indian textiles sent to the Ottoman Empire was about five times more than that transported by the British and the Dutch.[24] It is only because of the nature of the sources available to us today that we know more about Ottoman–European relations than we do about Ottoman–Mughal ones.

But that is not all. One can provide illuminating instances of these exchanges between the Ottoman, Safavid, and Mughal empires, while staying in the domain of textiles, to show that they touched on other levels. In addition to trading relations, there were exchanges of artisans, techniques, ideas, and fashions. Unfortunately, what we now know of this subject tends to be piecemeal until further research is undertaken, but, nevertheless, it is clear that such exchanges were significant and that their impact was directly on the regions concerned and also worldwide.

For example, within a large territory, there were artisans who traveled from one town to another, carrying their skills with them to new places where they settled to work and where they helped to form new guilds. These artisans were in all likelihood relatively few, since as a general rule, artisans tended to be sedentary. Nevertheless, their impact helped to diffuse textile techniques from one location to another. Textile designs inspired by Persian and Indian cloth were imitated in Aleppo, Cairo, and Istanbul, as confirmed by numerous sources. For instance, during a visit in Istanbul in the 1760s Jean-Claude Flachat, a French entrepreneur who lived in Istanbul for some years, observed that following the troubles in the Safavid Empire, many Persian artisans established themselves in Istanbul, where they introduced the methods of Persian cloth to the Ottoman capital; in the Aegean island of Chios, artisans had learned to imitate the Italian cloth sold in Istanbul and to introduce improvements to it. Many artisans learned to adapt their cloth to the demands of the destination where it was to be sent.[25] And according to Jacques Peuchet (d. 1830), cloth makers in Damascus and Aleppo were using cotton thread spun in India, while weavers were making cloth designed according to the style of Bengal.[26] Aleppo weavers were imitating the shawls of Kerman in Persia,[27] while the Indians imported textile techniques and dyeing techniques from the Ottoman Empire and from Persia.[28] And from the fairly distant city of Tunis, in the opposite direction, fez makers moved to Istanbul in the eighteenth century when this headwear became popular there.[29]

A similar picture could be seen in Egypt, with multiple influences and exchanges taking place. The *dimittes*, inspired by a kind of Egyptian cloth made in the Mediterranean port of Dumyat (Damietta), were imitated in Izmir, Sayda, and Cyprus.[30] In Cairo, artisans came from Diyarbakr and Bilad al-Sham and formed guilds that specialized in the Indian-style designs that were gaining enormous popularity in Europe and the Ottoman Empire; in eighteenth-century Cairo the wealthiest merchants, whose fortunes could be counted in the millions of paras, were those who dealt in India cloth.

At one level, these examples show how artisans moved from one place to another for a variety of reasons; they show the movement of techniques and of know-how in a large region where cloth production was of considerable importance; they also show a level of interdependence that touched the region. Finally, they shed light on the role of the anonymous artisans who were trying out new places and new techniques in their attempts to earn a living, and whose initiatives were an important factor not only in creating the multiple economic links within this region but also in the dynamism of its economy.

At a broader level, they raise another issue, notably the economic weight of this region, with its production, commerce, skills, and know-how. The vitality of the activities in this region, both productive and commercial, offers additional evidence for the perception of a multi-centered world from 1600 to 1800, rather than the unipolar vision of a Eurocentric world.[31]

More specifically, with regard to the potential effects on Egypt of the expansion of world trade, these have as yet to be fully recognized and understood. The secondary literature of Egypt's trading activities, to a large extent thanks to the work of André Raymond on the coffee trade and the trade in Indian textiles, has recognized the importance that Red Sea trade continued to have in the economy of seventeenth- and eighteenth-century Egypt, long after the settlement of the Portuguese in India.[32] Many studies have expanded on this theme. These have mainly focused on the nature of the trade, the trading activities of merchants and their relations to political authorities, the goods exchanged, the shipping patterns, the beneficiaries of this trade, and the networks. As a result, we probably know more about merchants and commerce in Cairo than in most other cities of the Ottoman Empire.

However, that represents but one aspect of the picture. By shifting the focus to a broader sphere, we see that Egypt fit into a more global picture of the period. From another angle, we can focus on the potential social, economic, and cultural consequences of this trade. This approach is useful since it shows trade not only as an exchange of merchandise but also as a vehicle for the movement of people, for the transmission of trends and patterns, and for the exchange of fashion and know-how. In short, trade was a vehicle for connecting regions to each other.

Interconnectedness, the existence of common regional and world trends

This raises some questions of how to understand Egypt in the context of world trade. One way is to consider the model of 'interconnectedness,' which some historians have identified as one feature of the early modern period. Joseph Fletcher was one of the early historians who considered this interconnectedness as a feature characterizing the early modern period. While it was evident that during this period, countries like India, China, France, and England each had its own history and its own specificities, he proposed to identify those trends that were roughly contemporaneous, that these countries had in common. The interconnections, continuities, and trends that linked them together were either a result of contact between them or in response to the same social or economic forces, even without direct contact.[33] A similar line of argument can be found in Christopher Bayly's work. One theme in his *The Birth of the Modern World* is that the growth of a more integrated society was a feature of nineteenth-century society. Prior to that, in the seventeenth and eighteenth centuries, which his book describes as 'archaic globalization,' there were networks that had been created by the geographical expansion of ideas from their local setting to more regional and international levels.[34]

Growing commercialization

Despite the absence of references to Egypt in these studies, a scrutiny of economic, social, or cultural conditions suggests that in some domains, the trends in Egypt had parallels elsewhere, in other parts of the Ottoman Empire, India, or Southeast Asia, or in Europe, and that it is very likely that these parallels, evident in regions that were quite distant from each other, were the result of a common factor that was experienced by them. One consequence of the extensive trade was that, in Egypt, as in many parts of the world, there was an accompanying expansion of commercialization. In an earlier publication I developed the idea of commercialization as one of the trends for which we could find parallels for what was happening in Egypt, India, and Southeast Asia.[35] This same theme is taken up in chapters of the present book and developed further. We can also observe them in the more concrete pattern of artisans moving between one region and another, taking with them their skills; and in more abstract domains, namely in language, we can observe in Egypt, various parts of Europe, and India a shift toward a written language closer to the spoken word. While this shows that a variety of different aspects could be seen as having an international dimension, it also shows that the conditions of this period were such that they created a kind of duality between those activities affected by world conditions and those that were less affected.

The worldwide expansion of trade led to an expansion in the use of money, a greater monetization. This was evident especially in the centers of trade and production where exchanges were frequent and intensive, and it could be observed in Egypt, Anatolia, and different parts of the Ottoman Empire. In the Balkans, for example, a study has shown that increasingly during the eighteenth century, inheritances left by people when they died consisted of cash rather than goods.[36] Sevket Pamuk has noted in his study of monetary history of the Ottoman Empire that, although there were periodic shortages of money, by and large, there was an increased availability of specie after the sixteenth century and an increased availability of coinage in the eighteenth century, thus facilitating the access of rural populations as well as artisans to easily available cash money.[37] It would be difficult to imagine how cash *waqf*s (pious foundations) spread in small towns in Anatolia among ordinary people unless there was easy access to cash that these *waqf* founders had beyond their immediate needs. In this form of *waqf*, persons endowed cash, which was lent at interest, and the interest served as income for the *waqf*.[38]

There are parallels for this trend elsewhere. Commercialization could also be observed in India, which was exporting more textiles to the rest of the world than any other country. Here too, the flow of money led to a greater monetization of the economy. Scholars like Frank Perlin have shown that monetization reached both urban and rural populations in India.[39] Likewise, the study that Anthony Reid undertook in his book on Southeast Asia in the early modern period shows that more and more, in places like Burma and Thailand, taxes were being paid in money rather than in kind, especially after the mid-eighteenth century. Moreover, it appears from a number of these studies that this monetization was reaching ordinary people rather than being limited to those who were directly involved in international trade.

There is another dimension of commercialization that seems to have become a trend, namely, that money relationships were penetrating noncommercial structures. Its manifestations are well known. In Egypt, as in many other parts of the Ottoman Empire, the latter part of the seventeenth century witnessed a trend in the sale of offices. A person who had been granted a position in a *waqf* or a salary in a military regiment could exchange the position against the payment of a sum of money.[40] Kenneth Cuno's work has shown that notables traded offices and positions against payment, as if they were a commodity, while the state tried to maintain its control.[41] We can see this commodification in the inheritances of the wealthy merchants like Sharaybi and of prominent religious figures like Shaykh Muhammad Shanan, who was Shaykh al-Azhar between 1711 and 1720. These inheritances included, among the commodities that their heirs would inherit, the wages for the positions that they had obtained, and which had been placed as if they were private property.[42] Such practices had by the eighteenth century become commonplace. Likewise, *iltizams*, or tax farms, were also subject to market transactions, since they changed hands in exchange for money.

Even in a traditional structure like the guild, which was not essentially a moneymaking structure, the eighteenth century witnessed a certain level of monetization in different parts of the Ottoman Empire. In Anatolia, guilds owned copperware, which was rented out in order to create funds for a number of purposes. Money could be lent to guild members who wished to expand their business. The interest on these loans went to charitable purposes such as helping poor members.[43] A parallel development emerged among some of the wealthier guilds in Cairo, such as textile guilds or the guild of linseed pressers. They likewise imposed fines as a punishment to members who violated guild laws rather than firing them from the guild; this kind of punishment became integrated into the guild rules. Prior to this development, the violations of guild rules were punished by nonmonetary means. For an artisan who wanted to be promoted to master craftsman, it was not enough to demonstrate the level of skill that he had. He also had to make a contribution in money or in copper to the guild in order to be promoted.

Possibly these money practices were inspired by the fact that, from about the mid-sixteenth century, the Ottoman state was using a system of fines as a substitute for the fixed punishments set up in the Qur'an. Fines rather than corporal punishment were commonly imposed for crimes such as theft or adultery. According to Sami Zubaida, such fines, which were explicitly prohibited by early jurists, became an important source of revenue for the state treasury.[44] These state practices provide one further example that money relations were becoming more prominent. In summary, the trend toward monetization took a variety of forms within the Ottoman Empire. It was affecting not only the state but also military persons, merchants, and even ordinary people.[45] It reflected the greater degree of monetization that was taking place worldwide.

Thus, in one form or another, this trend in monetization appeared in many parts of the world, in all likelihood linked to the extensive flow of bullion from America to Europe, where it was used in trade in the Mediterranean and in Asia, making specie available in considerable quantities.

The intense level of worldwide commercial exchanges had other consequences that touched various aspects of the economy and of culture. As commercial exchanges became more intense they were accompanied by exchanges, notably of ideas, trends, and people. Exchanges of technologies or the spread of similar fashions spread along trade routes. There are indirect indications that commercialization had an impact on society, since it tended to blur class lines. A more commercialized society was likely to encourage social mobility. It also tended to expand commercial culture. Peter Gran considered that the eighteenth century in Egypt witnessed a penetration of a utilitarian culture into the academic culture of the time.[46] This commercialization provided the context for the expansion of texts in vernacular Arabic, which in the seventeenth century was in the process of becoming legitimized.

Consequences of These Conditions

There were consequences to these conditions. One was manifested in the textile production in the seventeenth and eighteenth centuries, which provides a concrete illustration of the involvement of Egypt in the markets, trends, and fashions that were invading the world.

The local gains a global dimension

Textile production was a major economic activity, and Egyptian textiles were much in demand in foreign markets. This craft was more closely linked to outside markets than many other crafts, insofar as local artisans, through the intermediary of merchants, were responsive to changes in market demand and to international fashions, and they adapted the cloth they made accordingly. This is particularly evident in the spread of Indian-type designs, which were being imitated in many textile centers worldwide. Christopher Bayly noted, in his study on the emergence of the modern world in the nineteenth century, how people from very different cultural backgrounds, in many parts of the world, mainly belonging to elites, were starting to follow similar fashions.[47] Although he was referring to the nineteenth century, when European-style clothing was gaining popularity in various countries, in fact this trend can be traced to an earlier period, at a time when Indian cloth dominated the world textile trade. Giorgio Riello has shown how Indian textiles became a worldwide commodity. Not only was Indian cotton sold in practically all corners of the world, in Persia, Ethiopia, Congo, and East Africa, among others, but its techniques and designs were so popular as to be imitated in many textile centers in Europe, Asia, and the Ottoman Empire. Cotton production had in fact become a global enterprise.[48]

Indian-style textiles (*indiennes*, as they came to be known in French) were also being made in Istanbul, Diyarbakr, Aleppo, Cairo, and other cities in the Ottoman Empire. One of the first attempts to imitate this kind of cloth in Europe was undertaken in mid-seventeenth-century Marseilles, with the objective of limiting importation from the Ottoman Empire and the Levant.[49] To do this, the factory owners had the help of Ottoman artisans.

As Athanasios Gekas has suggested, the Ottoman Empire played an important role in importing textile techniques and designs from India and subsequently transmitting this technology to Europe, an intermediary through which the secrets of Indian textile production passed and then were transmitted to France and the Hapsburg Empire.[50] However, the Ottoman Empire, in addition to its role as intermediary between India and Europe, was also an initiator of its own technologies, in textiles and other domains, for which there was a demand in Europe, and which ultimately penetrated European industries and medical structures.

In Cairo, a number of guilds appeared that specialized in making cloth inspired by Indian models. The cloth they produced was intended for both the local and the international markets. The export of cloth from Egypt to France, as we know from French sources, underwent a significant increase in the eighteenth century. A large variety of Egyptian cloth, including cloth with Indian designs, was sent to French ports. Certain types of Egyptian cloth, presumably inexpensive or coarse, were consumed in a region as far away as the Caribbean, where it was intended to clothe the slave population. Hence the production of various kinds of cloth was responsive to demand in foreign markets and to growing market demands corresponding to the rise in consumerism. These conditions suggest a reconsideration of much that was written about the history of Islamic textiles during this period. The view that emerges when these are studied in terms of the economy offers a different dimension from that which at present dominates studies of textiles in the context of the history of Islamic art.

There were also less concrete manifestations of the potential impact of trade; commercialization could have an impact on social relations as monetary relations opened the way to more social mobility. Its impact could also be observed in cultural aspects of life as class lines became more flexible. One concrete manifestation of this impact is in a shift in language, specifically in a trend toward the vernacularization of language that became apparent around the seventeenth century. A large number of texts were written in a language that did not fully conform to the rules of proper Arabic. This period, roughly from the fifteenth century to the seventeenth century, seems to be a key moment in linguistic transformation in Europe, Egypt, and many parts of Southeast Asia. This vernacularization was accompanied by a shift toward the use of a written language that was closer to the spoken word.

This transformation took different forms, and there were many factors behind it in each country. Such a shift in written communication is much more than a linguistic issue; it has relevance in terms of historical development. A language change of this kind cannot be dissociated from its social context. The use of a level of language that was close to the spoken word was part of a profound transformation that was taking place, affecting society as well as economy. Vernacularization, whether in Europe, Egypt, or India, meant that people who were not part of the educational or religious elites could have access to the written word. Although each country had a variety of factors that led to this development (for Egypt see chapter 2), there were parallel consequences. It is nevertheless probably not accidental that they emerge at roughly the same time. It is unlikely that these changes were the result of one region influencing the other. Rather, one supposes that these different regions may have been influenced by a common factor, notably the growing commercialization that was touching so many parts of the world.

In Europe, the shift from Latin to Italian, French, and German is well known. The vernacular Bible appeared in the sixteenth century, making it more accessible to the ordinary Christian. The development of the printing press was a major factor that, together with the language, helped to realize this development in Europe. It became important to use a language that people outside the educational establishment could understand. It is from this period that we can date the emergence of scientific works written in the vernacular: those of Galileo (d. 1642) in the seventeenth century were written in Italian rather than Latin.

Less well-known is the shift, roughly at the same time, toward vernaculars in India. Sheldon Pollock's work indicates that roughly in 1500, writers in many parts of South Asia were writing in local languages for literary expression in preference to the universal languages like Sanskrit that had dominated literary expression for centuries.[51] We know, for instance, that Babur, who founded the Mughal dynasty in India in 1526, wrote his memoirs in a colloquial form of Turkic (a dialect of northeastern Iran).[52] Other studies also show that in eighteenth-century India under the Mughals, there were medical manuals written in Persian rather than in Sanskrit, another indication of vernacularization, which some historians have associated with the decline of the Mughal state.[53]

Less known is the shift in Egypt, and to some extent in Syria, of a written colloquial called Middle Arabic because it combines colloquial and classical language. Middle Arabic (written colloquial) has a long history, but it is nevertheless from this period that this particular register of the Arabic language was given a degree of legitimacy and that academic texts made use of Middle Arabic. Given the importance of the classical language and the social weight given to its correct use, this development was considered by many as negative. The classical language was the language of the Holy Book; and moreover, al-Azhar, as a center of learning, had a particular reputation as an institution with high skills in the Arabic language, sought after by students from different parts of the Islamic world.

The trend toward the vernacularization of language, which has been studied as an individual phenomenon with respect to one language or one region, gains by being studied as a more general trend that had some significance worldwide. By changing one's angle of observation, certain elements come to light which can form part of a complex, multi-sided picture of change.

The factors behind the development of Middle Arabic in seventeenth-century Egypt are discussed in some detail in the first chapter of this book. Suffice it to say that in addition to those factors specific to Egypt, one cannot ignore the broader context, which shows a parallel trend in Indian and Persian languages and also in European languages. Of the multiple factors that shaped this worldwide trend, the one that many different regions had in common was the commercial conditions that prevailed. Egypt was subject to the same world trends that were apparent in many other countries.

Transfer of know-how

There are other ways in which we can identify the position Egypt had in the transformations of the period and potentially also in the development of modern world history. The intensification of trade was accompanied by an expansion in the exchange of know-how and technology, and such transfers were exchanged between the Ottoman, Safavid, and Mughal states. A further dimension relates to exchanges in the direction from 'non-Europe' to Europe. Recent scholarship about India, Indonesia, and South America shows that during the centuries from 1500 to 1800, there was a considerable flow of knowledge from these countries to England, Spain, and the Netherlands. In the various countries where Europeans went, the know-how that they observed among the natives in numerous fields was often collected and recorded and, at times, integrated into European knowledge.[54] One noteworthy example is from the land surveys that the British undertook in India. These surveys were a combination of the know-how of the British surveyors, with their techniques and instruments, and the knowledge of the local inhabitants. Kapil Raj has shown how, in the seventeenth and eighteenth centuries, the British in India tried to chart the geography of their territorial acquisitions to defend their borders, assess potential tax revenues, and ascertain the safety of communications. For this they had to rely on indigenous staff members and their skills. According to Raj, in the 1760s, when this was being undertaken in India, the British had no experience of countrywide terrestrial surveys, and there was at the time no countrywide detailed survey of the British Isles.[55] The resulting product was consequently a hybrid combination of the know-how of the British and the Indians. This train of thought is inspiring a number of other scholars to pursue research along the same line.[56] Chapter four of this volume elaborates on this subject.

For Egypt, the secondary literature has covered two aspects of these transfers of know-how with Europe. The most developed works concern the rule of Muhammad Ali (1805–48), whose policies of reform in numerous domains included both the integration of European know-how and the hiring of European experts in various fields. When Muhammad Ali established a new school system he was inspired by the French *lycée* system. When he established new hospitals, it was a French doctor, Antoine Barthélémy

Clot Bey, who headed his project. The factories he built employed skilled workers from various countries to run his projects. His grandson Khedive Ismail (d. 1895) went along the same road when he built the Opera House of Cairo in 1869, designed by Italian architects. The list is long and it has been relatively well covered in scholarship on the period.

The other aspect regarding transfers between Egypt and France is centered on the Napoleonic Expedition (1798–1801), which aroused immense interest about Egypt in France. The so-called 'Égyptomanie' resulting from this interest came to inspire all the arts.[57] The influence of Egypt and Egyptology on French culture was many-sided and touched various domains of French cultural life. But it was less the contemporary Egypt of the nineteenth century, and certainly not Ottoman Egypt, but rather pharaonic Egypt that French culture was interested in. As a result of the expedition, a surge of interest in Egyptology followed. The fashion for things from ancient Egypt came to permeate various arts in France, such as furniture, Orientalist painting, women's fashion, and graphic arts.

So much for the visual arts, about which we have a rich secondary literature that examines the multiple aspects of Egyptomania. The subject at hand is more mundane, and much less written about. It has to do with economy, a subject with none of the exotic qualities that Europeans often hoped to find in the Orient. The object of interest was technological know-how of textile dyes, or how to dye textiles with colors that were bright and would last, about how to learn techniques that were used on a daily basis by cloth dyers in Cairo and to implement them in France. This time, the transfers were from south to north, from Egypt and other parts of the Ottoman Empire to France.

The level of expertise in some aspects of textile production was such that the techniques of artisans were transferred to France and incorporated into some of the most important French industries. Thus, the technological and scientific knowledge that was transferred between Europe and non-European parts of the world was a two-way street. This chapter considers the transfer of technical/scientific forms of knowledge, of which we know little, or the transfer of techniques from Egypt to Europe, that had a bearing on French industrial production, the techniques of cloth dyes. Even though the working methods may have been 'traditional,' the artisan practices detailed here show how developments of the eighteenth century were at the base of some developments in the nineteenth century. These developments were from the base up, rather than the top-down developments that characterized much of the nineteenth century.

In the light of the developments that were taking place in other parts of the world, the transfer of dyeing techniques from the Ottoman Empire and Egypt to France and Europe were part of a global trend of transfers of know-how from one region to another. These south-to-north transfers can be put in context with numberless other transfers of technology and know-how that circulated during this period. Thus the circulation of this knowledge from different sources and in different directions was part of a pattern that had become fairly common during the early modern period.

This approach to the subject of textiles has a number of consequences. First of all, it means that we need to reconsider one of the dominant views about the history of textiles in Egypt, which portrayed the sixteenth to eighteenth centuries as a period of decline. This description of the production of textiles in the later period was current among art historians, who viewed this from a different angle. For them it is not the best or the only way to describe textile production of the seventeenth and eighteenth centuries. Textile production was probably creative at all times, albeit in different ways.

Second, it means that we need to reconsider the subsequent period in the light of these developments. It questions the idea that Muhammad Ali's policies of reform and industrialization were undertaken on a tabula rasa. Instead, it shows that we can make links between eighteenth-century textile production, undertaken in a traditional context by artisans, and the nineteenth-century factory production using wage labor. One of the more successful textile factories that he established produced cloth with Indian designs. Clot Bey, in the first half of the nineteenth century, writes that this factory produced eight hundred pieces of high quality *indiennes* a month and could compete with those produced in Germany and England, so much so that the imports to Egypt of this cloth are said to have accordingly decreased.[58] Possibly the workers in this factory were trained within the guild system; possibly too some of their techniques were transposed to the factory system.

The issue here is that the factories founded in the early nineteenth century on a European model may have integrated local practices. The production of these *indiennes* was well developed in Cairo before the appearance of the factory, and they were export items that were in demand. One detects here a kind of hybridity, or the existence of two systems of production that were essentially different, one of them linked to the factory and the other one linked to the artisan tradition. Likewise there were two sources for the creation of the modern factory, one of them based on European expertise and the other on local practice. Important as this subject is, academic research on it still has a long way to go.

Conclusions

To return to the question posed at the beginning of this chapter, finding alternatives to Eurocentric histories of non-European regions, the present study builds on the growing literature that searches for alternative ways to rethink the Eurocentric approach to the history of non-European regions of the world. This means that we need a history of Egypt that can integrate the developments taking place worldwide during this period. One can sum up the answer in a few points.

First, it is important to understand the period prior to colonial domination in its own terms rather than as a prelude to colonialism, and to understand how it fits into a global context. Such an approach to the history from 1500 to 1800 offers the historian several advantages. One is an alternative to the Eurocentric paradigm of "the rise of the west," by showing that Egypt, many other regions in the Ottoman Empire, India, and Southeast Asia were part of a number of worldwide trends, and that some of these were at the source of later developments. Egypt, like many other so-called 'Third World' countries, was in some way or other part of the process of formation of modern world history, since some of the features outlined above would have ultimately contributed to the emergence of the modern world. The idea that Europe had an exclusive role in creating the modern world can, as a result, be placed in a different perspective. Thus, this approach allows historians to make a link between the early modern period and the modern period, showing that what became a dominant trend in the nineteenth and twentieth centuries had roots in the period before. Consequently, one can reassess the links between this period and subsequent developments of the nineteenth century.

Second, on the methodological level, one point that the present book raises is that modern world history was not only the creation of academicians, intellectuals, or scientists. World history has often been expressed in macro terms, tracing broad lines of trends that had a broad impact on significant parts of the world. The material in this book traces some of these broad lines, such as commercialization; it also brings into the picture the ordinary people who either felt the consequences of these changes or initiated changes of their own. Many of these were artisans and their guilds, who initiated, innovated, or adapted ways of doing things, not in laboratories, but rather in an empirical way through their daily practice, through trial and error. In Egypt, this can be observed at the macro level as well as the micro level, with artisans and guilds in their daily practice: increased exchanges, expanded markets, and increased consumerism led them to bring changes to their work.

The absence of well-known names of great scientists or intellectuals whose output was transformative tended to emphasize the picture of decline. The study of east–west technological transfers allows us to see things down to up, not only through great men or intellectuals but also through anonymous persons. The book brings into the picture some of the initiatives undertaken by ordinary people, showing both how these initiatives could be part of significant historical processes, and how regional and world conditions could impact the lives and work of some of these people. Often at the source of modern science there was a local traditional craft that could eventually be integrated into the more universal world of science.

Thus, at more than one level, Egypt can be considered as a player in the formation of our world today. On the concrete level, one can cite the example of the contributions it made to technical know-how in cloth production, which penetrated and helped to develop modern textile industries in France. It constitutes one of many examples of know-how that was developed in the non-European world that contributed to the formation of the modern world. One can turn the focus away from Eurocentric narratives by redressing the balance toward a narrative that includes such contributions. These contributions can be considered part of a down-to-up process whereby the knowledge and techniques that artisans had created on the basis of practice rather than in the abstract or by use of a scientific method became incorporated into modern technical or scientific programs or products.

At another level Egypt was part of a process whereby the interconnections created by the conditions of the period led to similar types of practices adopted by distant regions. As the world became more closely knit, trends, practices, techniques, and fashions became, in the nineteenth century, more globalized. This process led to a greater level of standardization of numerous practices in the following century. What was taking place inside Egypt from 1500 to 1800 cannot be dissociated from its role in the construction of modern world history. Had there not been a dynamism and flexibility in society and economy, as well as initiatives that were undertaken by writers, thinkers, artisans, and tradesmen, it is hard to believe that it would have participated in this way in the developments of the later period.

2 Seventeenth- and Eighteenth-century Texts: Colloquial in Language, Scholarly in Form

Language Registers: What Did They Signify?

This chapter explores a phenomenon that developed in seventeenth-century Egypt: the emergence of many written texts that combine more than one language register, namely classical Arabic and the colloquial. Linguists call this language register that combines the classical and the spoken language or the vernacular and includes elements of both of these 'Middle Arabic.' These texts in Middle Arabic tended to include parts in standard Arabic and parts in a language close to the spoken word or at times substandard language. Middle Arabic has a long history, since it is used in some of the earliest papyrus texts, but during this period, its use in Egypt was considerably expanded from about the beginning of the seventeenth century.

Between the seventeenth and the end of the nineteenth century, there was a significant body of works written in Middle Arabic on a number of subjects, both literary and scholarly. This development has not received much attention except from specialists in Arabic literature and from linguists who have tended to see it in a negative light. Scholars who study Arabic literature have linked the expansion in the use of written colloquial to an age of decline (of both language and literature), during which the rules of classical Arabic language were ignored. The use of written colloquial was seen as a distortion of the correct language. This view was usually based on a comparison with the literature of earlier periods like the ninth and tenth centuries, which had seen a flowering of Arabic literature.[1] Thus the decline of language corresponded to a general decline of society after the medieval period, which touched many aspects of culture. A number of reasons were suggested to explain these changes in the written language. One of them—often put forward—was to explain the decline of language by a lack of interest on the part of the Ottoman governors. Another one was the poor performance of al-Azhar, which should have preserved and protected classical Arabic. A third explanation was the general cultural decline of the period.

These negative views have meant that until this day, scholars have studied the texts combining the classical language and the colloquial with the objective of pointing out the 'mistakes' and correcting them.[2] When manuscripts were published, what was considered to be substandard Arabic was corrected before it went into print. It has also meant that the texts written in the seventeenth and eighteenth centuries have not aroused the interest of historians, literary historians, or linguists, because they were associated with a literature in decline. There are exceptions, of course, like Madiha Doss, who has tried to combine her qualifications of linguist with a historical content.[3] She has recently published, with Humphrey Davies, an anthology of works written in the colloquial language, which includes a number of texts dating from the Ottoman period.[4] But by and large, the linguists who worked on such texts have focused on technical aspects, and their approach is consequently different from that of historians. Finally, whereas historians of the Ottoman period today hardly make use of the decline paradigm that dominated historical scholarship a few decades ago, scholars of literature and of language have not quite abandoned it.

There is much to be gained by studying language as an element in historical development and considering it as source material for understanding aspects of society. We can explore language as a factor to shed light on a period and to observe the interplay between history and language. This can add a dimension to our understanding of the period. Thus, when I observe changes in language, these are not explained in terms of linguistic theory or linguistic models, but in terms of the social, economic, cultural, or political conditions of that particular time. Such changes require us to think in terms of multiple factors, both local and regional. Changes in the way that language is used do not come alone; rather, they are part of a wider picture with many interconnected elements. What interests me is that social context can shape language.

Thus, for a historian, the question is to try to find out why, at certain moments, one can discern a shift in the way that language is used, and how such a change is linked to or caused by the historical context of the time. One can agree with Sheldon Pollock when he writes that the meaning of language change, in this case a shift toward the use of a level of language close to the spoken word, goes beyond the field of language or of linguistics. It may be linked to the changing boundaries of culture, society, and power, to changing perceptions.[5] It is along this vein that I would like to examine the language shift toward an expanded use of written colloquial, notably, to place this trend in a context that takes into consideration the broad historical developments, local and regional, that might have had an impact on the development of language. The expansion in the use of Middle Arabic was linked to the political and economic changes of the period; its consequences touched not only the language of texts but the structure and their content as well. It was not solely linguistic change, but a shift in cultural vision that affected the forms of writing.

Study of the expansion of this register of language gives us an added dimension to our understanding, showing that developments in language that were understood to be innovations of the nineteenth century need to be understood in the context of developments of the seventeenth and eighteenth centuries.

The geographical region covered by this book is roughly Egypt and, to a lesser extent, Bilad al-Sham (Greater Syria). It is possible that the trend traced here could have a broader application to other parts of the Ottoman Empire that underwent similar or parallel conditions. One has to wait until further research on language transformation is undertaken in order to establish connections.

The Prehistory of This Change

The interpenetration of colloquial and classical Arabic in written texts is not new. There were many reasons for its appearance. Prior to the seventeenth century, people wrote texts that integrated words, phrases, or sections in the colloquial level. Such texts have a long history. The earliest extant Arabic texts, the papyrus deeds of the eighth, ninth, and tenth centuries, provide us with an early example of writing in which the vernacular language has penetrated texts in the classical language. Over the centuries, its use could expand or retract. And, most important, because it was linked to specific contexts and conditions, it could be used for different objectives during different periods. The use of colloquial in written texts, moreover, had a number of forms.

At the time of these early texts, in the 800s and 900s, the process of Arabization had not been completed. The language of many of these papyrus deeds, in fact, suggests a level of Arabic that was not fully mastered by the writer. For some people, the language of the spoken word could be the only medium of communication with which the writers were familiar. Either they were not fully literate, or they were not fully knowledgeable about the Arabic language. People used the language as best they could, at their own level of familiarity, since it may not have been their first language.[6] This meant, of course, that the writing might include mistakes of various kinds. At times they did not follow the proper rules of grammar; at other times they used vocabulary which was not Arabic but incorporated elements of the original language of the writer, in this case, Coptic. When Arab armies conquered regions where many different languages were spoken, it is likely that the local languages of these regions made their mark on Arabic. In Egypt, with regard to vocabulary, Coptic words have entered the Arabic language, and studies of the papyrus documents of the early Islamic period show that they entered into both legal documents and historical narratives.[7] In Ibn Khaldun's (d. 1408) words, the Arabic used in North Africa incorporated elements of the Berber language while in the Mashriq, Arabic was influenced by Persian and Turkish, and in Andalusia, the language of the Franks had impacted the Arabic there.[8]

The use of substandard language in written texts could also reflect the writer's level of education, if for instance he was semieducated. This would be the case for people who had undergone elementary education, but for whom texts did not form part of their professional activities. There were other reasons for the use of the colloquial in early texts by persons who were well educated but chose to write in a combination of the two levels, moving between the classical and the colloquial, because of the nature of the subject matter, such as in a humorous or light text. There are some excellent examples of early letter writing, such as those published by Werner Diem, which illustrate this level of language with its grammatical irregularities close to the spoken word. The personal or spontaneous nature of some of the letters was a reflection of a person expressing his or her feelings. The letter written by a wife admonishing her husband on account of his infidelity is an example of a text that incorporated elements of the colloquial.[9] Likewise, in the popular literature of the thirteenth to fifteenth centuries, it was often the nature of the subject matter that pushed writers to incorporate elements of the vernacular language into their texts, even when they were familiar with classical Arabic. One example is the poetry of Ibn Sudun (d. 1464). Ibn Sudun was a second-generation Mamluk and a trained theologian, and clearly knew how to write correctly. He was nevertheless, according to Arnoud Vrolijk, reputed to be a buffoon and a hashish addict.[10] By nature a nonconformist, he was writing humorous verse, and the colloquial-style language that he wrote was well adapted to the subject matter: it was light and it was funny. Moreover, Ibn Sudun was himself considered an anti-establishment person, and consequently, his use of nonstandard Arabic was in keeping with his behavior and with the subject matter of his work. It was a statement through which he positioned himself in relation to his society, both through the language and through the content of his writings. These are some of the features of Middle Arabic in the period before the seventeenth century. There is subsequently a considerable expansion to written colloquial. To understand this change, one needs to trace long-term factors that may have impacted this language change, and to see it not in terms of linguistic development but in terms of factors that had an impact on society and culture in general, and by consequence, on language.

Why was there a shift in the written language around 1600?

A complex set of short-term and long-term factors, both political and economic, were behind the shift toward a greater role for the colloquial in written texts around 1600: the expansion in commercialization; the relationship between state and society; and the nature of the power structure, as these developed gradually over a long period. Some of these factors were local or regional and others were linked to world conditions. A subtle interplay of these factors could sway the balance toward either the local (Middle Arabic) or the universal (classical Arabic). These factors touched a number of domains in life. One was language. The following pages will focus on some of the important landmarks that led to this development.

The Landmarks and Their Consequences

The fall of the Abbasids—a push toward the vernacular

The fall of the Abbasid Empire in 1258 was an important landmark for the whole region. It was a major geopolitical transformation, affecting numerous populations and having an impact not only on politics but also on culture, worldviews, and language. One of its consequences touched religious life. The Abbasid caliph had for a long time represented the universal dimension of Islam, holding together the *umma* or Muslim community, at least at the symbolic level. The creation of smaller political entities left a mark on the worldview. The caliphate had provided a certain centrality; its demise meant a weakening of this symbolic image. It also meant that the Islamic community did not share the same political borders, as numerous political entities sprang up in former Abbasid lands.

Geopolitical changes affecting culture

This transformation had a number of cultural and social consequences. In a number of domains, there was a balance toward the local, as eyes turned toward a closer proximity. This was manifested in religious life, in historical writings, and even in some aspects of jurisprudence where, according to some scholars, what was local emerged with a greater visibility in relation to what was universal. Language fell into this same circle, as local dialect came to have a larger presence in written texts.

One dimension of the shifting balance toward the local is religion. As the caliph's unifying and universal dimension was fading, there emerged in numerous localities, both urban and rural, a multitude of local saints, shrines, and places of pilgrimage that became central to the lives of local people. And as the image of the caliph as a central figure in Islam faded away, it was these local saints that ordinary people turned to, and it was the local holy men that they sought for advice.

It is not accidental that the lifetime of many local saints corresponded with the cataclysmic events related to the fall of Baghdad and the penetration of Mongols into Islamic lands. Many regions were devastated by their advancing armies, leading many people to leave, searching for new lands to settle. A wave of Sufi saints moved from east, where the Mongol armies started their invasion, to west, many of them to Egypt, where the relative stability of the Mamluk state was an added inducement for them to settle there. In Cairo, Alexandria, Tanta, and Upper Egypt, many of these holy people found both security and refuge; numerous disciples found support in them and were ready to follow them.[11] Many of the most famous local saints of Egypt lived during this transformation: 'Umar ibn al-Farid (d. 1235), Ibrahim al-Dusuqi (d. 1296), Ahmad al-Badawi (d. 1276), Abul Hajjaj al-Uqsuri (d. mid-1200s), Abul Hasan al-Shadhli (d. mid-1200s), and many more. This is an indication of the profound effect that the fall of the caliphate had in the geostrategic balance of the region and on the lives of many people. With time, the number of saints and shrines expanded considerably. The study that Catherine Maycur-Jouen and Nicolas Michel undertook of a region in the Nile Delta, based on the register of the Rizqa Ihbasiya, a cadastral document dated 1527–28, identified around thirty-seven villages in which there were a total of about a hundred saints. This heavy concentration of saints and shrines indicates not only a significant expansion in the villages of the Delta, but is also a testimony of the very local nature of these holy men.[12]

At a time when the region was undergoing a major political reordering, and the caliphate and a caliph, reduced in stature, had become attached to the Mamluk state in a somewhat ceremonial capacity, for many people, these local saints and holy persons, close by and concrete, came to form the center of the religious lives of particular localities. Shrines were built for them, which became places of pilgrimage, and some, like Ahmad al-Badawi in Tanta and Abul Hajjaj al-Uqsuri in Luxor, have remained the patron saints of their towns up to this day.

Even though in the fourteenth and fifteenth centuries the caliph continued to retain some of his universal image as a symbol of unity among

Muslims, regardless of where they were, and even though, in Mamluk ceremonials, he was given a choice position, there was, especially among ordinary people, a shift toward the saints or holy men who were local, that the population could interact with, whose advice they could follow, and whose shrines they could visit. A similar trend was taking place, in different degrees, in Iraq, Syria, and Anatolia. Everywhere, shrines were built for holy men; local saints appeared in villages, rural areas, and towns. They became a focus for religious life.[13]

In academic writing as well, we can see the consequences of a shift of vision from universal to local. In what may seem to be an unrelated trend, we find another manifestation of a changing worldview, notably in the writing of histories and chronicles, which seems to have had a long-term impact. The fall of the Abbasid caliphate in 1258 created new conditions as the former territories of the empire were fragmented into smaller political entities. With this new political situation came a way of seeing the world more locally. We can see this in the histories that were written during this period. The Abbasid Empire had produced universal histories like that of al-Tabari (d. 923) or al-Mas'udi (d. 956).[14] Subsequently, as the political borders retracted so did the vision held by historians. Instead of the universal histories, there is a trend to write chronicles dealing with specific regions or cities: *Tarikh Makka al-Musharaffa* by Muhammad Muhammad Makki (d. 1480),[15] *Tarikh al-Quds* by al-'Ulaymi (d. 1522),[16] *Tarikh Hums* by Muhammad al-Makki (d. 1722), *Husn al-muhadara fi tarikh Misr wa-l-Qahira* by Jalal al-Din al-Suyuti (d. 1505),[17] and *Bughyat al-talab fi tarikh Halab* by Ibn al-Adim (d. 1262).[18] These are a few examples from a large body of works dealing with local histories. This trend was particularly obvious in Syria, where many cities had their histories recorded, as compared to Egypt, where histories tended to focus only on Cairo. In either case, the historians' vision was focused on a reduced geographical area, often the city where the historian lived.[19] Later histories were rarely universal, as the focus turned toward a single city or territory. Typically, the Mamluk histories and chronicles of the fourteenth and fifteenth centuries were about the territories that were controlled by the Mamluk state, even though the focus by and large was on the persons and events of Cairo. Even more

Cairo-oriented was al-Maqrizi's *Kitab al-khitat*, which described the city street by street and building by building, offering a history of each one of these. In fact the book is like a repertoire of the major markets and buildings of the city in the lifetime of the author. With these are intertwined the events and persons who had a connection to the buildings. The organizing principle of the book was urban geography rather than historical chronology.

The shifting balance between the local and the universal manifested itself in the domain of jurisprudence. This shift went around the role of custom or practice, by definition local in nature, in relation to Islamic law. Islam emerged in the Arabian Peninsula but spread across large regions of the world. Muslims living in these regions, regardless of language and ethnicity, came to believe in its message. In theory, Islamic law was universal and applicable to Muslims regardless of their language or ethnicity. In the period from the sixteenth to the eighteenth centuries, the universal dimension of Islamic law is complemented, at times confronted, with a theory on the weight that should be given to local custom.

The classical legal theory of Hanafi law elaborated in the eighth and ninth centuries did not recognize custom to be a source of law, even if, in reality, it may have been practiced in courts of law. According to Noel Coulson, "the classical legal theory does not recognize customary practice."[20] Yet by the sixteenth century, this theory seems to have been undergoing change. The statements made by a number of later scholars indicate that custom, or *'urf*, was indeed being integrated as a source of Hanafi law. The person whose name stands out for having elaborated a theory which justified the role of *'urf* or practice in Islamic law is the Egyptian Hanafi scholar, Ibn Nujaym (d. 971/1563).[21] The principle he upheld was that custom or practice, including even local practices undertaken within a restricted community, was a valid source of law, and was considered as legal within that community, even if it was not universally practiced by Muslims elsewhere. Ibn Nujaym considered that it was acceptable for a qadi to judge a case on the basis of the practice of a certain community, even if this practice differed from universal practice. Consequently, the *'urf* practiced in Cairo was as binding as law to the inhabitants of Cairo only; it did not have universal applicability.[22]

"Whatever is dictated by custom *('urf)* is as if dictated by law." A local custom had the same weight as a legal text.

Sometime later, Ibn Abidin (d. 1836), a Syrian scholar who lived in Damascus and was a well-known authority in Hanafi jurisprudence, specified that *'urf* or custom could change between one period and another, so what mattered was the custom of a particular community at a particular time. He also made a distinction between *'urf* or custom that was followed by all of the members of a particular community and *'urf* that was specific to certain groups *('urf khass, 'urf 'aam)*.[23] The seventeenth- and eighteenth-century religious scholars in Bilad al-Sham, like Khayr al-Din al-Ramli, mufti of Ramla, studied by Judith Tucker, likewise gave local custom a certain space when they issued their fatwas.[24] The idea of the value of local custom, in other words, was being discussed by scholars who wished to integrate it into the theory of Islamic law.

These different scholarly discussions of custom as a source for Islamic law are relevant for the weight and the consideration they give to local practice. Quite as relevant is the timing of these opinions, which emerge when, in other domains, an increasing value is given to what is local. True, this was a debate that was undertaken by academics, in works that were unlikely to be read by anyone other than academics. Yet, when placed in the context of other parallel developments along the same line, it takes on another significance as part of a broad trend linked to the reordering of the region after the fall of Baghdad.

These different examples in various seemingly unrelated domains are manifestations of a similar phenomenon, a broad cultural transformation which had touched the region, bringing about a shift in balance from universal to local. This cultural shift can be considered one factor in favor of a language shift toward the use of a written language that made more or less abundant use of the colloquial. Language, in other words, was subject to these same trends, and consequently local languages, or dialects, appear to have been given more weight and to appear more often in written texts. The shift in language usage coincided with a number of other changes in culture, constituting one dimension of a deeper transformation taking place in the region.

The manifestations in written texts

How was this manifested in the writings of the period? Margaret Larkin, in her study of literary texts, has found that from the thirteenth century, popular poetry frequently used colloquialisms, often mixed with standard Arabic.[25] One of the best-known and most studied thirteenth-century writers in this vein is Ibn Danyal (d. 1311), an oculist who was born in Mosul and moved to Egypt, presumably fleeing from the aftermath of the Mongol invasion. He was the author of three shadow plays, of which his *Tayf al-khayal* (The Shadow of Spirit), which narrates a Mamluk campaign in Cairo against vice, was the most important. His work was deeply rooted in social reality, depicting low life in thirteenth-century Cairo. The text was partly in classical Arabic, but he also used the colloquial for satire and for obscenities; he also used it, often in a satirical way, to express difference from authorities and the establishment. He was antiestablishment, and his use of language was an extension of his views.[26]

In summary, the level of language, such as that used by Ibn Danyal, reflected more than his individual leanings or his stand in relation to the establishment. Like the other social, political, and legal trends, language was adapting, in its own way, to the transformations taking place that were modifying the contours of people's visions.

Empire and language

Another significant landmark in the penetration of colloquial into written texts emerged as the fifteenth century developed. This time too it was linked to empire, in this case the Mamluk Empire (1250–1516/17), which ruled over Egypt and Syria. Like its predecessors, the Mamluk state had created its own language to reflect power. And with the Mamluk dynasty, not only was there a language of power, but this language was also a model of high culture.

The classic example for this level of language can be found in al-Qalqashandi's (d. 1418) *Subh al-A'sha*, written at the beginning of the fifteenth century. Manuals like that of al-Qalqashandi were considered part of the training of prospective scribes in the chancery. Most of these manuals consisted of instructions on how to write chancery documents. A scribe working in the chancery, in addition to many other skills, such as financial skills and accounting, should not only have a perfect command of the language but should also be eloquent. Belles-lettres constituted a major part of the scribe's training. When al-Qalqashandi, himself having worked in the Mamluk chancellery, wrote *Subh al-A'sha*, his book was intended as a manual to provide a model for apprentices, with the objective of achieving "unsurpassed mastery of the language" and of eloquence in writing.[27]

The Mamluk state became the most powerful empire of the Islamic world. It brought about a considerable development of the administration into a highly complex and structured body. One of the most important departments of the administration was the chancellery (Diwan al-Insha). It had not only its rules of conduct but also its language of power, which reflected hierarchy and high culture. In other words, the language of administration was associated with empire. The few extant published letters that were issued by this *diwan*, even in the late fifteenth century, maintain the rules of hierarchy of language. John Wansbrough's publication of a letter from Sultan Qaytbay (d. 1496) to the Doge of Venice shows the importance given to stylized language, which included lengthy honorific titles and high prose.[28]

Writers and thinkers of the period reiterated similar views on the ideal man of letters. Thomas Bauer's survey of Mamluk literature has shown how Ibn Nubatah (d. 1366) defined the ideal features of the *littérateur (adib)* as a person who had to be an expert in language, classical texts, and poetry. He was very similar to the ideal *katib* that al-Qalqashandi had described in his *Subh al-A'sha*.[29] There were also parallels between the language used by al-Qalqashandi and deeds that were issued in his time (fifteenth century), as was demonstrated by Emad Abou Ghazi: the influence of the court on the writing of these deeds, and the numerous epithets and praises that accompanied a person's name as a sign of deference—long and complex, but at the same time, in conformity with a fixed protocol which reflected hierarchies of power.[30]

For a long time, the Mamluk Diwan al-Insha, in addition to being an important government administration, also set a standard for writing. It was the model for literary prose style, and its men the prototype of the literary educated person. Language was associated with power, and with empire; the way that scribes wrote their official letters reflected the power of the sultan. The importance of language in power relations in general and in the chancery and administration in particular reflected the power of empire.[31] The language used in Diwan al-Insha can be associated with high culture.

A turning point in relation to the penetration of colloquial in written texts came about with the disintegration and demise of the Mamluk state. Toward the mid-fifteenth century, as the weakened Mamluk state went from crisis to crisis, there were frequent complaints that the administration was employing inappropriate people who did not have the right qualifications; they did not have sufficient education and sometimes they did not belong to the establishment, but entered the positions from the rank of artisans. Richard Mortel has illustrated this trend by following a coppersmith, Abul Khayr al-Nahhas (d. 1459), as he climbed the ranks of bureaucracy until he became, in the words of the historian Taghribardi, the most influential person in the realm.[32]

This was symptomatic of other changes. The hierarchy, which had placed the so-called 'men of the pen' at the top layers of the administrative structure, also started to erode, as less qualified persons entered the ranks, until with the end of the Mamluk period, their role was minimized. Likewise, for the Mamluk chancery, the end came in 1517, with the Ottoman conquest of Egypt; its functions were terminated and transferred to Istanbul. Thus what had been a model for literary prose writing ceased to exist. The people who had been professional writers of this high language decreased considerably as the bulk of the imperial administration was now taking place in Istanbul. For those who continued to practice, either in the much reduced Ottoman administration of Egypt or privately with important or wealthy persons, they also lost social status. The chronicles of the seventeenth and eighteenth century hardly mention them at all, whereas the fourteenth- and fifteenth-century chronicles contain innumerable obituaries of the men who worked in these departments.

The fall of the Mamluk state in 1517 coincided with the rise of an Ottoman imperial culture in Istanbul as the apparatus of the state and of its administration was transferred from Cairo to the capital of the empire. After the successful military campaigns undertaken by Sultan Selim (d. 1520), who conquered Egypt and Syria, and Sultan Sulayman (d. 1566), the Ottoman state administration in Istanbul was expanded and became more complex. It was accompanied by a parallel development in the domain of writing, a reflection of the association of empire with writing and language. The number of Ottoman chronicles increased as the Ottoman Empire became more firmly established. Under Sultan Sulayman, the court chronicler became an official position. Numerous histories were written, like that of Kemalpasazade (d. 1534), whose ten-volume history covered ten sultans; possibly the most important of these court historians was Mustafa Na'ima (d. 1716).[33] The late sixteenth-century chronicles, as Christine Woodhead's work has shown, used a rhetorical literary style strongly influenced by Persian literature and were intended to reflect the "voice of the court."[34]

The development in language which was taking place in the capital of the Ottoman Empire during this period seems to have been in the opposite direction to what was happening in Egypt as the centralized rule of the Mamluks was coming to an end. In Istanbul, a more formal language was emerging by 1600 from its earlier base of the colloquial Turkish of Anatolia. The Ottoman language was in the process of developing into a prestige language of administration and literature. It was a language that was in keeping with the needs of the empire and of its administration, polished, formal, and meant for a restricted audience. It was a reflection of power and of hierarchy. In addition to this, those who moved in the courtly circles were expected to know the Persian language and to have a literary education so that they could appreciate poetry and belles-lettres.

Thus, toward the end of the fifteenth century, the Mamluk Empire, with its strong hierarchy and its emphasis on ceremonial and on language as manifestations of this power, was gradually starting to erode. The move of the capital of empire from Cairo to Istanbul meant the transformation of Cairo from capital of an empire to capital of a province. The symbols, the manifestations, the hierarchies of power and of empire, lost some of their strength.

The consequences of this change were many. One of them can be seen in the writing of chronicles. Mamluk historical chronicles, which Tarif Khalidi has rightly described as "imperial bureaucratic chronicles," combined historical knowledge with power.[35] Chronicles that were written at the beginning of the fifteenth century usually listed, at the beginning of every new year, the names of the dignitaries occupying the high state positions, in a hierarchical order, starting by naming the ruling sultan and moving down to the important state personages in descending order. Hierarchy was very important. By the beginning of the sixteenth century, Ibn Iyas's *Bada'i' al-zuhur* no longer does this, because the hierarchy had disintegrated. Benjamin Lellouch's study of the last years of Mamluk rule and the first years of Ottoman rule, as narrated by Ibn Iyas, traces a change in language linked to the erosion of the Mamluk power structure. The loss of this hierarchy led to an expansion in the use of direct speech. Direct speech and colloquialisms became more frequent as Ibn Iyas progressed in his narration of the fall of the Mamluk power structure.[36] The work of two other late fifteenth-century authors of chronicles likewise moved between classical and colloquial, al-Sayrafi (author of *Nuzat al-nufus*), who blended colloquial and formal usage, and Ibn al-Himsi.[37] These late fifteenth-century writers were harbingers of what was to come, namely the writings of the subsequent centuries in general and the chronicles in particular of the seventeenth and eighteenth centuries, which made much more abundant use of the colloquial.

It would seem that this becomes a dominant mode of historical chronicles in the following centuries. As these became dissociated from empire, there is a shift of both content and language. With the lessening of the weight of empire, the vision of the authors of chronicles was taken in other directions. The chronicles that were written in Egypt and in Syria during the seventeenth and the eighteenth centuries were no longer imperial chronicles; they were not intended to be a reflection of imperial power. As a result, the way they portrayed society also changed. There was a tendency to focus on the ordinary and the everyday events of ordinary people. This is especially true of Syrian chronicle writing. We find examples in the work of Ibn al-Tawq (d. 1509), a Syrian notary who lived in Damascus at the end of the fifteenth and the beginning of the sixteenth century. There is a greater presence of first-person narrative. Ibn al-Tawq reports the family quarrels of his acquaintance; he informs his reader that his wife and children went to the public bath *(hammam)*.[38] His work was both a personal diary and a record of the public events to which he was a witness. In it, he recorded many private events about friends, neighbors, and family; a lot of what he wrote was close to the spoken language. There is a certain informality in the way that he writes that seems to be adapted to writing in the colloquial.

It is also evident in the writings of later Syrian authors, like al-Budayri al-Hallaq (d. 1762) and Ibn Kannan (d. 1754), in different degrees. The histories record public events of a political nature such as the accession of a new governor, or a natural disaster like an earthquake or the start of a plague epidemic. The new element is that they also record, with great frequency, events of a more private nature. They write of the death of a relative, of an outing with friends, of a family visit.[39] Al-Budayri al-Hallaq, himself a barber, interspersed his work on the history of Damascus, which covered the period 1154–75/1741–62, with news about other barbers, including his own master, who had taught him the barber's craft, and, now and then, news about the guild of barbers of Damascus. And Ibn Kannan, together with his recording of public and political events, also included in his history information of a more personal nature, informing his reader that the preacher's son was getting married, a wedding that he was invited to attend; his own son getting married and the invitation he issued to his friends; his visit to his friend Abu Yusuf Ali where he spent five nights and enjoyed the blooming of roses while he was there.[40] There are, in other words, references to oneself and to one's family. Evidently, such a context was conducive to more personal writing. And more personal writing was conducive to the use of more informal language. For some of these writers this meant that the language register moved down a level; it became closer to the spoken word, even at the expense of correctness or polish.[41]

Another landmark, language and commerce

In addition to these local and regional factors, there were also some global factors, emerging in the period 1500–1800, that had an impact on the way texts were written.

The shift in language that we can observe in Egypt around 1600 was part of a much broader transformation touching many countries. It had parallels in a number of other regions of the world, all occurring at roughly the same time, that is, within the two or three centuries between 1500 and 1800. The development can therefore be linked to the worldwide transformations that were taking place during these centuries and that were affected, some directly and others indirectly, by the expansion of world trade. With regard to India and South Asia, Sheldon Pollock in particular has shown that in many parts of South Asia, by 1500, writers turned to the use of local languages for literary expression in preference to universal languages (such as Sanskrit) that had dominated literary expression for centuries.[42] The political, economic, and cultural contexts that were behind such a shift away from Sanskrit had their parallels in Egypt and Syria, as Middle Arabic expanded and gained a degree of legitimacy. From the sixteenth century onward, and more especially during the eighteenth century, there was a worldwide expansion of long-distance trade. With regard to Egypt, there was a considerable increase in transit trade in eastern goods, namely coffee, which became a popular commodity everywhere, and Indian textiles, also in great demand in the Ottoman Empire and in Europe. The immense fortunes that merchants could make from the trade in coffee and Indian textiles placed them high in the social ranks.[43] There was also an expansion of trade in local commodities. All this meant that directly or indirectly more people were involved in trade. It also meant that the greater the volume of commerce, the more important bookkeeping became. Peter Gran has argued, referring to eighteenth-century Cairo, that there was a link between the development in a commercial culture and the expansion of a utilitarian dimension in academic culture. The expansion of commercial activity could have an impact beyond the economy, specifically on culture and social structure.[44]

In many regions of the world, the expansion of trade was one of a set of factors that was associated with shifts in language toward vernaculars. This process of vernacularization that we detect in Egypt had parallels, roughly at the same time, in other broad regions of the world. As was the case for Egypt, each had its own specific factors behind this shift. Languages that were linked to religious writings, like Latin and Sanskrit, were being replaced by local dialects. In Europe, the vernacular Bible came with the spread of Protestantism in the sixteenth century; it was followed by many other works written in French and Italian rather than in Latin. For example, scientists started to use vernacular languages in the sixteenth century. Jacques Peletier wrote a book on algebra in French in the mid-sixteenth century, while Galileo (d. 1642) wrote his work, *Discourse*, in Italian. These were possibly attempts to reach a larger readership and disclose useful information, rather than to keep it secret as was the earlier practice. At roughly the same time, in India, many writers were turning to the use of local languages rather than the universal Sanskrit when they wrote literary texts, while Sanskrit, like Arabic, continued to remain the language of communication for academic writings. There was a move toward the vernacular, but scholarly or scientific texts were consistently maintained in Sanskrit while literary texts used the vernacular.[45]

Much the same situation applied to Arabic. Classical Arabic at all times remained the dominant form of written Arabic. Texts using a combination of classical and colloquial never replaced the classical language. Moreover there were certain types of texts, namely those of the religious sciences, which were invariably written in classical Arabic. The shift from classical to Middle Arabic is one of proportion, notably that a significantly larger portion of texts on various subjects made use of this register of language.

This trend toward vernacularization seems to have cut across borders. It had parallels in regions that were relatively distant from each other, that were not necessarily influenced by each other, but rather were subject to the same influences.

These are some of the factors behind the unusually important expansion of Middle Arabic that occurred sometime at the end of the sixteenth or the beginning of the seventeenth century. It was symptomatic of deep changes in society. This form of written communication was socially inclusive rather than exclusive. One can thus take this to be a reflection of certain social transformations.

Impact on Language around 1600

From the beginning of the seventeenth century and for some time thereafter, one can observe a number of developments in the way that Arabic was used in written texts. The penetration of colloquial in these texts not only spread considerably; it also came to be used in a variety of writing types and genres and by various social groups, including by persons who were part of the educational establishment. It gained legitimacy as a means of written communication. This meant there was a broadening of possibilities in the way language was used for written communication. It also meant that written communication became more accessible to social sectors that were not part of the establishment or the educational elite. And the expansion of an accessible level of language broadened the possibility of writing about the ordinary: ordinary people and ordinary subjects.

Thus the trend toward accepting texts that made use of colloquial as a legitimate means of communication dates from a much earlier time than that suggested by Shmuel Moreh. Moreh claimed that Arab writers in the modern period started to use colloquial expressions or local dialects under the impact of European literature. For him, writing that used colloquial only gained legitimacy fairly late, since popular literature and folk literature were despised in classical times. He associated it with nineteenth-century modernity, and he claimed that the source for this modernity came from Europe.[46] The history of texts in Middle Arabic was longer and more complex than is suggested, and the legitimacy that it attained some two centuries earlier was certainly at the source of the developments that he referred to at the end of the nineteenth century.

In these various regions of the world that were affected by trade, a more commercial culture might allow a kind of flexibility between scholars and nonscholars, which could, in turn, have an impact on the world of writing. In the course of the next two to three hundred years, there is a somewhat larger presence of persons outside the establishment who were using the written word. In Syria as well, a series of histories were produced in the eighteenth century that were not written by ulama.[47] One of these is the barber mentioned earlier, who in the eighteenth century wrote a chronicle about Damascus. In Cairo, an herbalist/doctor is presumed to be the author of a heavily colloquial seventeenth-century treatise on crafts in Cairo.[48] There is a series of eighteenth-century chronicles written in Cairo called the "military chronicles" or the Damurdashi chronicles, thought to have been written by men in barracks. Daniel Crecelius has noted that the Damurdashi chronicles were written in a style that made use of the colloquial language, with numerous grammatical and stylistic mistakes and misspelled words, but that they nevertheless used numerous words borrowed from Turkish and Persian, implying a certain level of education.[49] Madiha Doss also studied the language of the Qinali manuscript, one of the so-called "military chronicles," and concluded that the limited educational level of the writer was evident through his misspellings and sentence structure; possibly he had not gone beyond elementary schooling, that is, the *kuttab*.[50] This indicates a range of variety in the way that the colloquial penetrated into written texts, from the text written by a well-educated person who chose to write a colloquial that was combined with correct classical sections, to a kind of colloquial that had the features of substandard language.

In a related development, the writings of the period show a certain propensity to dwell on the ordinary. This means we find references to everyday people and everyday subjects, a development which in itself would be conducive to using unsophisticated language close to the spoken word. We also find, as was recently stated in an article by Rachida Chih and Catherine Mayeur-Jouen, that introspective writing was closely linked to medieval and Ottoman Sufism in Egypt, a trend that seems to have undergone a certain expansion in the eighteenth century.[51] Personal writing and self-narratives were not limited to Sufi works. They are dispersed in passages in different kinds of writing. Autobiographical accounts can be found in dictionaries, biographies, and histories, dispersed among other kinds of information, narrated in a language close to the spoken word.[52] A similar development in Europe, in the form of the multiplication of letter writing, autobiographical texts, diaries, and self-narratives, has been attributed to the Protestant Reformation and the Enlightenment, to the emerging state, and to the spread of literacy and books.[53] To these one could add the spread of a more intense form of commercialization.

This situation nevertheless was a source of tension between those who stood for the maintenance of a purer and more classical form of language, or for a language that was universally understood by the users of Arabic, and those who, on the contrary, stood for a local form of the language, which offered broader access of the written word and was less concerned with correctness. The tension is manifested in indirect ways in some of the texts of the late sixteenth and early seventeenth centuries.

The genres using the colloquial

Far from the theoretical debates for or against the use or the inclusion of the colloquial, there is a significant expansion of the use of texts that combined classical Arabic and the colloquial. This expansion is particularly evident as various forms of colloquialisms penetrated written works of a scholarly genre. Dictionaries were but one of these scholarly genres. Other kinds of writing that were influenced by this shift toward the colloquial were histories and chronicles; to a lesser extent, colloquialisms and dialect can occasionally be found in some of the deeds registered in court records.

Proliferation of dictionaries of the colloquial

One of the striking features of the period was a flourishing of interest among scholars in the colloquial, manifested by an unusually large number of dictionaries dealing with it. Much earlier on, as a reaction to the changes brought about by the influence of foreign languages and foreign words on Arabic, there appeared, as early as the ninth century, dictionaries that identified these foreign words with the objective of weeding them out, considering them as corrupt forms of language. They identified foreign terms in order to guide readers toward the proper Arabic vocabulary with the objective of keeping the classical Arabic language in its pure form.

For several centuries after that, few colloquial dictionaries were written. Then, starting toward the latter half of the sixteenth century, they again emerged in relatively large numbers. Radiy al-Din Yusuf ibn Hanbal (d. 971/1563) wrote a dictionary criticizing the language of the *'amma*, or commoners.[54] Yusuf al-Maghribi (d. 1019/1610), by contrast, wrote a dictionary in defense of colloquial. Al-Bakri was the author of a shortened version of al-Maghribi's dictionary of terms used by Egyptians *(ahl Misr)* which concorded with the Arabic language.[55] Shihab al-Din Ahmad al-Khafaji (d. 1659), scholar and qadi,[56] and Muhammad Amin al-Muhubbi (d. 1111/1699) also compiled dictionaries.[57] In two of these dictionaries, the point of reference, as the titles indicate, is the speech of the inhabitants of Egypt, and they vary in their attitudes between approval (al-Maghribi) and disapproval (al-Muhibbi).

Of these various dictionaries, the most interesting for our purposes is that of Yusuf al-Maghribi (d. 1610), author of *Daf' al-isr 'an kalam ahl Misr*, a text recently published by a Dutch linguist, Elisabeth Zack.[58] Al-Maghribi, who started out his life as an artisan, as he tells us himself, is particularly significant in this context. He was familiar with the marketplace; he knew the vocabulary that was used by different craftsmen when talking of their work techniques and work tools. At the same time, having left his craft and studied Islamic sciences at al-Azhar, he had a foot in the world of learning; he knew Turkish and Persian and he moved in elevated social circles, attending their *majalis* or literary sessions. But when it came to language, his position was clearly for that form of language that was flexible and accessible. His dictionary was a defense of the spoken word, or the dialect of Cairo.

This concentration of dictionaries within a relatively short time is significant; so is the fact that it reflects a debate on the value of colloquial versus classical, a reflection of the tensions between local and global. The debate can be interpreted in more ways than one. On a broad level, it could be a manifestation of the shift to local, since colloquial was by definition a local form of speech, versus the classical that was in theory comprehensible to Arab speakers wherever they were. It could also reflect the tension between a broad commercializing trend of the period supported by those who wanted to see a level of language that was more accessible to larger numbers of persons, that was more informal and flexible, versus a more traditional trend supported by the establishment, by those who opted for a more exclusive and purer form of language. Several dictionaries concerned with the colloquial appeared within a relatively short span of time, reflecting the weight of a growing commercial culture, as witnessed by the expansion of written colloquial or Middle Arabic, and of the concern that this trend represented in a certain sector of society, with its supporters and its detractors.

It was often said that there were no chronicles or histories of any significance written in Egypt between Ibn Iyas at the start of the sixteenth century and al-Jabarti at the end of the eighteenth. Peter Holt disagreed with this statement and wrote a short article in which he enumerated a number of historical chronicles and histories that were written during these two centuries. He nevertheless pointed out that the quality of most of them was poor, both in their content and usually in their language as well. In fact, it was not so much a matter of the absence of chronicles, but of their quality.[59]

One of the issues that has raised concern among modern scholars is that many of the Ottoman chronicles were written in substandard language or made use of colloquial more or less extensively. Some scholars concluded for this reason that they were not worth publishing. A number of manuscripts were published only after their language had been corrected.

Among these is the so-called anonymous "Paris Fragment" on the history of Ottoman Egypt in the seventeenth century that made wide use of Egyptian colloquialism and shows, according to Kamaruzaman Yusoff, an inadequate grasp of classical Arabic. Yusoff reaches similar conclusions with regard to another anonymous chronicle of the same period, entitled *Zubdat ikhtisar tarikh Misr al-mahrusa*, filled with Egyptian colloquialisms and inconsistent, sometimes erratic, spelling.[60] The histories that Peter Holt called "popular chronicles" were in his words "ashamedly colloquial";[61] he referred specifically to al-Ghamri's *Nuzhat al-iʿlam* (c. 1630) as being written in "atrocious verse."[62] Even the greatest historian of the eighteenth century, Abdul Rahman al-Jabarti, who along with his father was closely linked to al-Azhar, did not always follow the correct rules of grammar, made use of colloquialisms, and even used slang, which remains apparent even though in the course of publication his language was 'corrected' by editors.[63] There are more of these, but they are not published and are not known to many historians except from the catalogues of Arabic manuscripts.

Court deeds

Another kind of writing where we find written colloquial is in court records. Most cities of the Ottoman Empire have court registers where the daily dealings of the qadi were recorded. These registers contained a great variety of legal documents: litigation and disputes, marriage contracts and issues of personal status, *waqf*s, and notarized deeds of various kinds. One would expect these legal documents to be in the proper classical language. The scribes working in the courts who wrote the court cases were trained to use certain legal formulas. Manuals called books of *Shurut* offered guidance on how to write the different kinds of court cases, the formulas, and the vocabulary that court scribes had to learn for their profession. The scribes were expected to be familiar with the rules in these books and to follow them when they wrote the court cases, whether these were marriage contracts, sales or rent contracts, pious foundations, or disputes.

An examination of court registers indicates that these formulas were indeed closely followed in the deeds. There were set ways to write a marriage contract, for instance, with a formula on the way to start the contract, the data that the deed should contain, and the end formulas. The contracts that are recorded in court registers repeatedly use this model. However, what often happened was that the deed followed the set formulas in the introduction and in the conclusion, using the proper format and language. When it came to the content, there was often a difference in the level of language used. Some court cases contained vernacular, at times, and occasionally direct speech.[64] This was especially evident in cases of litigation where the plaintiffs made declarations. Court cases moreover included non-Arabic words that were borrowed from Turkish and had become Arabicized, like *oda* for 'room,' or words in Arabic that used a Turkish ending, like *khurda*, *khurdaji*. Although no systematic study of the language of court records has been made, it seems that the practice of including colloquial words and phrases was not uncommon.

A number of scholars have noted that court records in different parts of the Ottoman Empire made use of substandard language now and then, but there have been no scholarly studies of this trend nor have there been any attempts to consider it as a regional trend. Jon Mandaville, for instance, notes that the Arabic court records of Syria and Jordan contain colloquial words and usages while the Turkish language cases contain inconsistencies in spelling, morphology, and syntax, which the author attributes to clerks who had a weak grasp of the Turkish language.[65] Sometimes, when the court case reported the direct speech of a plaintiff, a vocabulary that was vulgar and obscene was recorded in the mouth of a speaker, such as in a case dated from 1049/1639 recorded in the court of Beni Suef in Upper Egypt, where a man accuses another man of having insulted him. "He called me a pimp, a son of a bitch," "*ya 'ars, ya ibn al-qahba, ya mufalaq*;"[66] and he told his wife, "If you leave the house and go tonight to sleep at your mother's house, I will triple divorce you."[67] These direct quotes, although they were not very frequent, when they nevertheless were recorded in court cases, tended to be close to the spoken word.

In short, after 1600, colloquialisms were frequently present in historical chronicles, court records, official letters, government documents—that is, in almost every kind of writing with the exception of texts in Islamic sciences, such as jurisprudence, traditions, exegisis, and so on. It had spread to academic as well as nonacademic genres of writing and had become an acceptable form of written communication.

Innovations in the Way Colloquial Is Used

Al-Maghribi's innovative methodologies

Innovative features can be traced to the period around 1600 and are particularly important in the history of written colloquial. The works of two authors illustrate these innovations: al-Maghribi, author of the dictionary of colloquial mentioned earlier, and Yusuf al-Shirbini, the author of *Hazz al-quhuf*, one of the most famous works of the late seventeenth century. Through these we can see some of the innovative ways they used written colloquial and the new methodologies they adapted to the use of this language.[68]

Dictionaries of colloquial that were written in the ninth and tenth centuries aimed at identifying words that did not have an Arabic origin—that is, the words that entered the language as the Arabs spread to non-Arab lands—with the objective of cleansing the language from what was foreign *(dakhil)*. Early dictionaries called *lahn al-'amma* appeared with the objective of maintaining the purity of the Arabic language. The dictionary of Yusuf al-Maghribi did the opposite. Al-Maghribi wrote his colloquial dictionary with the objective of legitimizing the colloquial, an important innovation. Just as significant was that his opinion of colloquial was supported by his methodology. To this purpose, he used a methodology that was somewhat different from that of classical dictionaries. In classical dictionaries like those of Ibn Mandur and Firuzabadi, when the definition of a word was given, the author provided the reader with a number of references to earlier definitions to support his own. The word was defined in the light of how earlier dictionaries, such as those of Jawhari or Firuzabadi, defined it.

Even though al-Maghribi often referred to such classical dictionaries as that of Firuzabadi, he also used, in addition, his own techniques for defining words. For him, the source for his work was the language as he heard it, that is, as it was spoken by people, regardless of whether or not it corresponded with the academic language of books. Al-Maghribi followed this method, but in addition, he also based his definition on "that is what I heard" or "that is how they say it." His source for defining the word was the spoken language, or language as it was used, not only as his predecessors had defined it. This methodology allowed him to make distinctions between the vocabulary used by Egyptians, the one used by Maghribis, and the one that Turks were using. A word could have a particular meaning when a person from Cairo used it and an entirely different meaning when a person from the Maghrib used it. This method also allowed him to make distinctions between the words as they were used by the *khassa* and as they were used by the *'amma*, in other words, the vocabulary according to class: all of this being based on what he heard as his reference. Hence, we have not only a new methodology for the way to study language, but we also see a clear change in attitude. The academic method was innovated in order to give credence and weight to the spoken language and to link it to the text that was written in this easier form of expression.

Al-Shirbini's *Hazz al-quhuf*

The other seventeenth-century writer whose work in written colloquial stands out is Yusuf al-Shirbini. When we talk of colloquial during this period, there is one work that everybody knows, a work written around 1660 by Yusuf al-Shirbini, entitled *Hazz al-quhuf*. Everyone who studies Arabic literature knows about it. It is a very large book of several hundred pages and has been published several times in several editions, including a recent edition and translation in two volumes undertaken by Humphrey Davies. It is one of the very few literary works of the seventeenth and eighteenth centuries that has been published or studied, since the majority of such works are still in manuscript form. For a long time, scholars have pointed out that *Hazz al-quhuf* is a unique book, because it is entirely about peasants in the Delta part of Egypt, a unique subject matter, and because of the colloquial language that it uses. We now know that the use of written colloquial was far from being unusual in the seventeenth century, and that it was commonly used in various kinds of writing, literary as well as academic.

Nevertheless, this work does remain unusual, even unique, even in the context of the numerous texts of written colloquial that we have. For one thing it is long, close to 450 pages in a recent edition, and certainly the longest work to be written in this language register. According to Humphrey Davies, who edited and translated this last edition, *Hazz al-quhuf* can be considered "the richest pre-nineteenth century source for the study of Egyptian Arabic." Davies found close to seven thousand passages in colloquial.[69] Although the internal information in the book indicates that the author was an educated man, had been to al-Azhar, and was familiar with important works in Arabic, he used more colloquial than most of his contemporaries.

This work is also innovative because it includes many passages of direct speech by peasants, what some scholars believe is a peasant dialect, with peasant vocabulary, and different from the Cairene dialect used in the other colloquial passages. Al-Shirbini claims that he used two kinds of colloquial: one was the spoken language in the city and the other was that of the countryside.[70]

An analysis of the developments since around 1600 shows that there is more than one level at work. The first is the explicitly articulated debate expressed by those who favored writing in colloquial or who thought it had the same value or weight as classical Arabic. They were few. Yusuf al-Maghribi stands out as an early spokesman for this trend. About a century later, Muhammad Hasan Abu Dhakir, a writer of belles-lettres, likewise took the same stand, in more explicit and stronger terms. In a literary piece of prose he wrote in about 1750, he explained that there were several positive aspects in colloquial and defended a freer type of language that expressed what the writer wanted to say. Abu Dhakir considered that language should be flexible and made to reflect meaning rather than follow rigid rules of correctness. For him, what really counted was the meaning that one wanted to express, rather than the correct use of proper forms. He consciously advocated freer expression and language neither tied to rigid rules associated with scholarly learning nor filled with the ornaments and embellishments of high literary canons. His view of colloquial went beyond the domain of language. For him, it was a social statement. It helped him to express where he stood and how he perceived those around him. He wrote at the colloquial level, using the sentence structure and the vocabulary of the spoken word, and he also theorized about it, albeit in a limited way. Abu Dhakir, in the eighteenth century, and Yusuf al-Maghribi, in the seventeenth century, were vocal, articulate, and thought that colloquial texts were legitimate.[71]

Although those who took a stand for the use of a flexible language were few, the level of practice presented another picture. People who were not familiar with al-Maghribi or Hasan Abu Dhakir were making use of written colloquial, perhaps for the same reasons expressed by these two, but also because they were subject to the forces of society that had helped to create the trend toward written colloquial: the shift toward local versus universal, the erosion of empire and the models of writing and of *adab* that the Mamluk administration had elaborated, and the expansion of commercialization linked to a greater level of world trade. Thus, as the seventeenth century was developing, some writers were paying attention to the language as it was spoken and were transposing it into the written word, elevating written colloquial to a degree of acceptability. When direct speech, colloquialisms, and slang reached dictionaries, chronicles, letters, and legal deeds, then we can say that, although in 1600 Yusuf al-Maghribi was the lone voice among language scholars, what was happening on the ground was a consolidation of his views about colloquial, so much so that one could say of the seventeenth century that it took written colloquial a step forward toward being a legitimate form of written communication.

Without attempting to link the use of written colloquial to specific groups, one can trace some trends in the seventeenth and eighteenth centuries.

Language and class

Beginning in the seventeenth century, Middle Arabic was related to class. The penetration of colloquialisms in written text continued to be characteristic of those with limited learning skills. But as this level of language gained legitimacy, its use spread among various classes of society.

Giants of the eighteenth century

In the eighteenth century, some of the great intellectual figures incorporated colloquial into their writings, indicating the establishment of this level of language as one of the standard forms of Arabic. This form, not identical to classical Arabic, was still the standard language for works on the Islamic sciences—*fiqh*, *tafsir*, Hadith—but nevertheless a form of language that, in works other than those in the religious sciences, had attained its own legitimacy.

At this time al-Azhar prided itself on its language studies, and students came to Cairo from other parts of the Islamic world to learn Arabic at al-Azhar; some of the best language specialists were teachers in that institution. What may seem like a contradictory situation to us today may not have been seen in this way by contemporaries. Otherwise it would be difficult to explain why some of these intellectual giants of the eighteenth century do not seem to have any compunctions in their use of colloquial.

One of these figures is Abdul Rahman al-Jabarti, author of *'Aja'ib al-Athar*. Even though he, as well as his father Hasan al-Jabarti, belonged to the class of high ulama, linked to al-Azhar, he used a language that contains numerous colloquialisms, despite the "corrections" of modern editors. Al-Jabarti records in his chronicle the poetry composed by some of his contemporaries, among whom was the well-known satirist Shaykh Hasan al-Badri al-Hijazi. Most of al-Hijazi's work is only known through al-Jabarti. Here too, the language of Hijazi made extensive use of colloquial and dialect phrases.[72] Al-Jabarti's chronicle sheds light on another phenomenon that was current in his time. He frequently refers to exchanges of letters between the various Mamluks, letters referred to as *tidhkara* or *maktub*. Rather than literary epistles, they were for the most part notes sent each other to inform them of a new development or news, or to warn them of a forthcoming danger. For instance, al-Jabarti narrates that at the time of the civil war of 1123/1711 between the Mamluk households, the various parties sometimes communicated information in writing, to stay home and not roam the streets, or to stop the fighting.[73]

Some of these letters have survived and are being studied with the objective of publication by Nasir Ibrahim. These are written in a form that makes use of colloquial. This makes sense since, first, not all Mamluks knew Arabic and not all of them were familiar with the classical, and second, from the way that al-Jabarti refers to them, one can infer that they were short notes, to the point, transmitting a piece of information to a friend or colleague, rather than polished letters that followed a set format.[74] In these various examples, the historian does not attempt to 'correct' the language that was used.

Another intellectual giant of the eighteenth century is Murtada al-Zabidi (d. 1791), a man of great learning and highly esteemed among Azhar scholars; he wrote a dictionary, *Taj al-'arus*, more of an encyclopedia than a dictionary, since it contains some thirty-eight volumes, the largest in the Arabic language. This dictionary is still considered a basic tool in the Arabic language, but unfortunately has not as yet been fully exploited either by linguists or by historians, in spite of the immense possibilities for research that it offers. Al-Zabidi, as demonstrated by Stefan Reichmuth, was a master of classical Arabic, with an unmatched command of Arabic philology. And yet, it incorporates numerous words in *'amiya*, probably close to a thousand words, as indicated in a recent publication by Rajab Ibrahim.[75] These were not only the *'amiya* or colloquial of Cairo, but also included colloquial words that were used in the many parts of the Arab-speaking world where al-Zabidi had traveled, such as Yemen, his country of origin. The dictionary is a reflection of his broad vision of the Islamic world and of the weight of the local dimension. Not only are colloquial words part of this dictionary, they are incorporated with no criticism; there are no negative comments stating that they are a mistake, and al-Zabidi does not suggest they must be corrected. Rather, he included them in *Taj al-'arus* because they had entered the written language, and he accepted their validity. Al-Zabidi's inclusion of words in *'amiya* in a dictionary that was to remain a standard dictionary for the next two hundred years must be understood in the context of the social and economic conditions of the time. His work was the child of developments that had occurred from the thirteenth century onward. This state of affairs lasted till the latter part of the nineteenth century.

These great scholars, who stood at the top of the intellectual and educational hierarchy, were not averse to integrating, in different degrees, elements of the colloquial in their writing. On the other side of the spectrum, ordinary people, who were not part of any educational establishment or who did not earn a living in the domain of learning, were naturally also making use of written colloquial.

Writings for 'ordinary' people

It is not likely that either Yusuf al-Maghribi's colloquial dictionary or Yusuf al-Shirbini's satirical piece on peasants was written to be read by ordinary people, even though the language used was much more accessible than classical Arabic. Both of them were relatively long works. Al-Shirbini's *Hazz al-quhuf*, in spite of its humor and satire, and its aim of entertaining the reader, had an intellectual dimension, even if this was not immediately obvious. Nevertheless, it appears that some of the texts of the period, written in colloquial, might have been intended for such readers, writings that were short, light, and accessible. We know, for example, that books of Juha jokes were passed on from the oral to the written form; books of anecdotes could also be found and might be considered light entertainment.[76] Their reading was relatively easy; they could be read out loud, for entertainment, to a group of people.

As further evidence about where and how written colloquial spread in the seventeenth and eighteenth centuries, certain writings, by their very nature, indicate that the readers were 'ordinary' people. These are writings for specific religious communities. One example is a prose narrative written in Arabic using Hebrew letters. Heikki Pelvi, a linguist who studied this manuscript, believes that it was based on oral literature that was common in Lower Egypt, and that it followed the style of professional storytellers, with the addition of a few Judeo-Arabic forms. The text contains very few classical Arabic phrases: the rest is in colloquial.[77] This piece is significant because it provides additional evidence that the written colloquial that was spreading in scholarly works, and in works intended for an educated audience, was also spreading among an audience that was not within the educated establishment—the Jewish community of Cairo, for whom this was intended, mainly consisting of traders and craftsmen.

The language was easy and the manuscript was short, some fifteen pages. Likewise, in the Coptic community, hagiographies were also written in Egyptian colloquial for the purpose of teaching the community, and were very probably read out loud to its members. These lives and stories about the martyrdom of saints were written in the forms of storytelling, using direct speech, at times creating a dramatic effect.[78] These texts, whether people read them or they were read out loud to them, used a language that the ordinary person could understand. The objective in using this level of language was to make the texts accessible to many people.

On the basis of these long-term developments, the assertion of a dichotomy between colloquial, the language of the uneducated or semi-educated, and classical, the language of the educated elite, does not hold up well. The developments that written colloquial followed do not support such a view. True, certain texts in classical were beyond the abilities of those without sufficient education; other texts bear testimony to the writing of semiliterate persons. But by and large, written colloquial, as it developed and spread, went beyond these class lines. These developments in the way that language was used were much more complex than a black-and-white picture of this dichotomy.

Where did these developments leave the classical Arabic language? The comments that James Grehan made about seventeenth- and eighteenth-century Damascus must certainly have also been true of Cairo. He writes that among the educated class, knowledge of the Arabic language, whether in conversation or in written texts, was highly regarded. Muhammad Khalil al-Muradi (d. 1791), a leading figure in the religious establishment of eighteenth-century Damascus, thought that an accomplished scholar should use a lofty and literate register of language, even when he was speaking (not to mention when he was writing), and he should be able to quote citations from the Qur'an or other religious scriptures at the appropriate moment.[79]

The expansion of texts that made use of dialect and colloquialisms had not pushed out the texts in *fusha* (classical Arabic), nor had they discredited them. They had widened the range of possibilities in language levels in use, a change that was supported by some and resisted by others. Hence their development was neither linear nor entirely straightforward.

Another Moment of Transformation: 1900

If one were to make a chronology for the history of colloquial writing, in which 1600 marked an important moment, as has been suggested above, then a second important moment emerged at the closing decade of the nineteenth century. Again, as in 1600, the tensions arose between a universally accepted form of Arabic and a local dialect, between acceptance and rejection of strict perception of its use. Once more, this development was linked to a power structure, this time the emergence of the nation-state. And once more, there were parallels as other emerging nation-states also underwent a similar development.

This moment represented a rupture of a trend that had been developing for some centuries and that had made of colloquial texts an accepted means of written communication. It was a rupture that led to the delegitimization of written colloquial.

At the end of the nineteenth century, there again emerged a debate about language, this one much more heated than the one that occurred about 1600. It involved many more people: writers, thinkers, politicians, and journalists. The debate revolved around the question of what language register to use, colloquial or classical Arabic: which one was acceptable and which one was not acceptable? The views were wide-ranging.

This tension was reflected in the growing newspaper business. There was a lot of discussion about the status and the future of the Arabic language by people like Butros al-Bustani in the periodical *al-Jinan* and Gorgi Zidan (1861–1914) in *al-Hilal*. For Zidan, writing in colloquial meant that if people forgot the correct Arabic, they would lose their heritage of thirteen centuries, since all these works were written in classical Arabic.

Many other writers and journalists thought that writing in colloquial had a positive value. It was a way of disseminating knowledge among large numbers of people and of enlarging the pool of readers. Some newspapers, like the *Muqtataf*, picked up on the debate in the early 1880s, stating that modern knowledge should be disseminated in a better way and that one way to do this was to write in a language medium that people understood so as to reach all classes.[80] At the same time, Ziad Fahmy notes that the last decades of the nineteenth century witnessed an unprecedented number of texts written in colloquial, especially with the spread of newspapers that used this language register, and many plays and poems as well. But he also notes the growing resistance to this kind of writing and that it became difficult to publish material written in colloquial.[81]

One form of resistance was the reappearance of dictionaries of colloquial, not like the one written by Yusuf al-Maghribi, but like the early dictionaries called *lahn al-'amma* that were critical of colloquial words. Their objective was to provide the correct alternative that corresponded to the classical vocabulary. John Baskerville has identified three such dictionaries that were published in the opening years of the twentieth century, written by Hasan Tawfiq, Muhammad al-Dusuqi, and Husayn Futuh and Muhammad Ali Abdul Rahman.[82] None of these are particularly well-known figures, but the fact that there is a concentration of such dictionaries within a short time is again indicative of the tension that was arising from the issue of language in the same way as it was in the seventeenth century.

At the political level, this debate came at a time when the Ottoman state was facing crisis, and it became obvious that it could not last in the same form as before. European penetration, in its various forms—political, military, and cultural—was posing a new threat to economic interests and to local identities. The question of language consequently took a political dimension. For many thinkers, reform and progress of the emerging nations became linked to the use of the classical Arabic language. The literary renaissance also became associated with a renewed concern about classical Arabic. To this effect, language academies were established at a somewhat later date, in Cairo, Damascus, and Baghdad. Their objective was to reinforce the Arabic language and its heritage. The success of the Arabic language was equated with the success of the Arab nation.

We can find parallels for this development in other countries where the development of the nation-state was accompanied by a standardization of language. This usually meant that local dialects had to give way to the language standards set by the capital or the center of administration. Most often, this was a change imposed from above. In France, for instance, *patois*, or local dialects, of which there were some dozen, became associated with the rural and primitive, with the rough and crude, as opposed to the rich and polished French language. In the opinion of the adherents of the privileged Parisian form, these dialects had to be replaced.[83] In England, likewise, calls were heard beginning in the eighteenth century to set uniform standards for the language. London English was seen as superior to the multiple dialects spoken in other parts of Britain, and consequently the model of language for the rest of the nation.[84] Policymakers who had a say in the state school systems, whether in Egypt or in these other countries, could also have a say in seeing that the proper level of language was taught. Local dialects became marginalized and associated with illiterates.

What this meant was a reduction in the number of language levels. Where there had been, for some centuries, a plurality of language forms, each with its level of legitimacy, by the end of the nineteenth century there was a reduction of these forms, so that one single form came to dominate. Ultimately what came out of these debates was that the written colloquial that had been current for a few hundred years was delegitimized, and has to a large extent remained so to this day. It was no longer an accepted form of written communication and was considered with disregard.

At the same time, supported by the spread of newspapers and elementary education—meaning more people were readers an easier form of Arabic developed that was more accessible than the classical Arabic, but different from the written colloquial that had been so prominent in earlier writings. The expansion of commercial presses and of newspapers and printed books required the use of an easier medium that was more accessible to larger numbers. A large sector of the written word was created outside of the religious establishment and by others than the ulama of al-Azhar. The growth of a middle class was another factor that supported the use of an easy form of the written classical language. In a different way and to a different degree, tensions continued between local and global.

The study of written colloquial development over the centuries has relevance for our understanding of the history of the period. First, it represents one aspect of what was a more general process toward the standardization of certain practices, for example, more homogeneity in language as in other aspects of life, like food and clothing. Second, common causes in various regions around the world had parallel consequences for the development of language, whether as a result of the intensive trade in the seventeenth century or of emerging nation-states in the nineteenth and twentieth centuries. Seen in this light, the developments in language were part of a broad historical process that had multiple consequences for the societies of the time.

3 Eighteenth-century Textile Artisans and Guilds and the World Economy

Artisans and Guilds 'Outside History'?

In keeping with the theme of this book, the present chapter considers the role of artisans and guilds in Egypt in the context of world history during the period from 1500 to 1800. It addresses the question whether we can consider guilds and artisans as part of this history or if they were 'outside history,' that is in a stationary state, autonomous, and unaffected by what was going on elsewhere. At a time when world commerce and world markets were expanding and when the world was becoming more interconnected, when these broad transformations were taking place on a global level, were artisans, guilds, and, most important, the products they were making in any way part of these changes?

These questions are easier to answer in relation to merchants than in relation to artisans. The merchants of Cairo who handled the Red Sea transit trade, spices, coffee, and Indian textiles, which were sent to numerous destinations around the Mediterranean and from there farther on, were quite likely to feel the consequences of the intensified commercial activity of the period from about 1600 to 1800. They had a quasi-monopoly over the Red Sea trade, especially when the coffee coming from Yemen that they handled ultimately reached distant parts of the world, not only in the Ottoman Empire but all over Europe, where it became one of the most fashionable drinks of the seventeenth century.

It is not difficult to see that merchants would feel the consequences of an expansion in world trade.

When we turn from merchants and their trade to artisans and their production, the picture is less clear and studies on the subject fewer. Views on the subject are divided. For a long time, scholars considered guilds to be structures that were static, restricted in their movements by state controls. They portrayed artisans and craftsmen as incapable of change, to a certain extent because they were governed by restrictive guild rules. For many historians, the guilds were structures 'outside history,' functioning regardless of their regional context. Early studies on the subject tended to emphasize the stationary character of these structures. Gabriel Baer, for example, who wrote one of the first extended studies on the subject, which remained influential for some time, considered guilds to be traditional structures bringing together persons of the same craft, headed by a shaykh. The guild was recognized by the state but was strongly influenced by state controls over its activities. The guild discouraged competition between its members but at the same time offered them fair treatment. Expansion of a guild was made difficult by restrictions for entrance, as a way of protecting its members from competition; persons who were not members of a particular guild were not allowed to undertake the activities in which it specialized.[1]

Since then, the emergence of court records as a major source for Ottoman history has given studies on guilds a great push forward. We have numerous books and articles on many aspects of guild history in the various cities of the empire, such as Cairo, Istanbul, Bursa, Damascus, and Jerusalem. As a result, we know much more about this structure than did the scholars of a generation earlier. This new scholarship shows that guilds were flexible structures; that there was enormous variety between them; that there were various models of the relationship between guild and state as well as between guild head and guild members; and that guilds could change their internal structure over time. As more studies were undertaken, it became clear that there were also differences between the artisans and guilds of one city and those of another. In Istanbul and in other Anatolian towns, for instance, the weight of the central state on guild activity was greater than it was in Cairo since, in the view of Timur Kuran, it restricted their room for maneuver and curtailed their development.[2]

More to the point is recent scholarship, which shows that links existed between eighteenth-century guilds and world conditions. One trend in these studies is the exploration of the way that guilds reacted in the face of the growing European threat. The economic and commercial rise of Europe in the eighteenth century is thought to have brought about an economic and financial crisis in the Ottoman Empire that led to a decline of guilds and production.[3] The importation of European goods had a destructive effect on the production of artisans, as did the exportation of the raw material that local artisans used in their work. Another trend shows how artisans and guilds, when they were threatened by the inflow of European goods, reacted to these crises by adapting their practices accordingly. Scholars have addressed this issue in different ways, but there is some agreement that the internal structure of guilds was affected by the prevailing conditions.[4] In her study of eighteenth-century guilds of Istanbul, for instance, Fariba Zarinebaf found that as the European threat increased, the Ottoman state took measures to protect guilds and merchants and could be seen as an actor on the stage and an agent of change.[5] Likewise, Caglar Keydar has traced an internal history for Ottoman guilds, suggesting that in the eighteenth century, there was a liberation from guild restrictions and a flourishing of rural manufacture at the expense of urban guilds.[6] These historians were concerned with the way that guilds adapted to changing conditions.

Building on some of these studies, my own work considers this subject from a different angle. Rather than understand the long eighteenth century as one during which artisans, faced with competition by European goods and with its economic penetration, were put in a difficult position to which they reacted in one way or other, it poses the question another way. The question is how do we place them in the context of world transformations of the period from 1500 to 1800, at a time when European hegemony had been extended to America and to parts of Asia but had not reached the Middle East or the Ottoman Empire. European merchants who were trading with Egypt and many other parts of the Ottoman Empire were looking for goods that they could purchase rather than markets for goods they could sell. The detrimental flow of European merchandise, which deprived artisans in the Ottoman Empire of their raw material, started earlier in some provinces of Ottoman lands than in others. In Izmir, for example, scholars date it from the eighteenth century.[7] However, for most other provinces of the Empire, and certainly as far as Egypt was concerned, this is not apparent before the mid-nineteenth century.[8] Only then did Europeans become producers of goods they could sell in these regions and buy raw material that was essential to local artisans. The time span covered here is prior to the emergence of this process. The questions that need to be addressed and nature of the debate are consequently different.

Unequal development

The expansion of world trade during the period 1500 to 1800 had an impact on local conditions in Egypt, touching several (but not all) sectors in society, both economic and cultural. This impact can be seen in domains like the circulation and exchange of information and know-how, commercialization, and vernacularization.[9] It is possible to discern a degree of globalization prior to the modern period, affecting a few sectors of society and economy. It was, in part, based on textile production and trade, on artisans and merchants, unlike the globalization of the modern period, closely linked to state policies and the rapid communication provided by steamship and railways. It did, however, leave many other sectors out, resulting in unequal developments between the different sectors of society, economy, and culture.

The unequal development of different sectors in society was mirrored in the broader picture of society at the time. The European capitalist penetration was also an unequal process which did not take place in all parts of the Ottoman Empire simultaneously. Nor did the connections to world trends touch all the social or economic sectors, at the same time or in the same way. The degree of change that these connections brought resulted in the emergence of hybrid forms and multiple patterns: changes, when they occurred, did so at different speeds.[10] One could consider this hybridity to be a characteristic feature of the long eighteenth century.

Turning from the macro-level to that of local artisans, eighteenth-century commercial conditions likewise had an unequal impact on guilds and artisans. The majority of guilds produced for a limited market. The guild of knife makers, the guild of nail-makers, the guild of needle-makers, those who made candles, and many more craftsmen produced their goods and sold them in the local market in relatively limited quantities.[11] Other artisans, because of the nature of their work, were more closely associated with world developments than others. Consequently these artisans and their guilds followed a particular trajectory, different from that of other guilds, in the structure of the guild and the organization of their work. Textile artisans and textile guilds were an advanced sector of the economy, with close links to world trade, and with a certain weight in the economy.

Textiles at the Vanguard of Change

Unlike what was happening in some parts of the Ottoman Empire like Izmir, where artisans who were confronted with an influx of European textiles faced serious problems, in Egypt, on the contrary, there was, in the course of the seventeenth and eighteenth centuries, an expansion in the production and the trade of textiles.

One reason is the link between textile production and the world market. For most of the period, the conditions of world trade worked to the advantage of textile production because the world market for cloth was undergoing a considerable expansion. In a recent study on the globalization of cotton textiles before the modern period, Prasannan Parthasarathi and Giorgio Riello have shown how after 1500, cotton cloth, the bulk of which was made in the Indian subcontinent, became the most important manufactured good in world trade.[12] Their study was meant to serve as a counternarrative to that of the cotton narrative, which was the basis of the Industrial Revolution in Britain. Their work showed how the cotton trade that originated in India extended to many regions of the world including Japan, China, Africa, and Southeast Asia. It also showed the consequences of this cotton trade. In Egypt too, even though the secondary literature rarely mentions it, there is evidence of an expansion in the production of textiles in keeping with this worldwide trend; this production found important markets in world trade. This subject, important as it is to our understanding of conditions prior to the nineteenth century, has not yet received the attention it deserves.

The expansion of world trade in textiles had numerous repercussions locally in Egypt among textile producers and textile guilds. It tied them more closely to the world market, a process by which they gained a global dimension that was to become reflected in the organization of their work, in the amount of textiles that they produced, and in the way that some of them reorganized their guilds. These artisans represent a sector that was more susceptible than others to the changes taking place in the world. It is therefore important to reconsider the mainstream views about the weight of the textile industry in Egypt and to rethink guild history in these times of change.

One manifestation of the economic weight of textile artisans was their relative prosperity in relation to other artisans. According to the study that André Raymond undertook of their inheritances, it is not a coincidence that textile workers and sugar producers in Cairo were on the top of the list, and that they left much larger fortunes than other artisans, sellers of vegetables, makers of pipes, or the numerous singers, dancers, and entertainers who left no inheritances at all.[13] The average inheritance left by a textile worker for the period from 1679 to 1700 was calculated as being of a little more than 50,000 nisfs (the nisf is the smallest silver coin), second only to the wealthiest artisans, the linseed oil pressers and the sugar producers. Their inheritances were somewhat above the average of the artisan population in general, calculated by Raymond as being above 48,000 nisfs.[14]

At a time when the textile sector was forging links to world trade, many other guilds tended to be restricted in space with regard to their practice, their networks, and their markets. Artisans are not known to have traveled much and, unlike merchants, did not have extensive networks. Most artisans produced a limited quantity of goods, and therefore their market was limited. Often, the geographical sphere within which they functioned was also restricted, sometimes within a single city and not farther than that. Sometimes artisans functioned within a single district in the city that was their home and place of work. Guild rules sometimes reinforced these limitations, restricting them to a particular district in a city. They were sometimes explicit about the geographical sphere within which its members could sell their product. The rules of the guild of bracelet-makers, for example, specified that any member of the guild who wanted to sell his wares in a town or village outside Cairo could only do so after having obtained permission from his guild head.[15] The local nature of many of these guilds is clearly illustrated in the work of André Raymond. He published a list of the guilds of Cairo in 1801, containing about 280 guilds, put together by the members of the Napoleonic Expedition. The list shows the local nature of some guilds, sometimes limited to one particular district in the city, for example, a guild of those who made iron chains in the district of Taht al-Rab' or a guild of sellers of sacks in Khan al-Khalili.[16]

This situation ultimately led to a kind of duality between those artisans and guilds that came closer to the world economy, adapting, in the process, their work and their guilds to these conditions, while at the same time many artisans maintained their close relationships to their guilds. Those less affected by world conditions and who practiced within a limited geographical sphere continued to follow the traditional path. Rather than talk of the history of guilds, one could talk of guild histories in the plural, in that, due to world conditions, there was more than one history of guilds. By following these developments in textile guilds, one can trace their path in relation to other guilds. The conditions of these guilds contrast with those of the textile guilds, whose sphere of activity was wider and whose products were diffused to many parts of the world.

Penetrating the International Market

In the seventeenth and eighteenth centuries, the cloth made in Egypt penetrated the international textile trade, reaching markets in four continents, Europe, Africa, Asia, and America. From medieval times, Egypt had an active textile trade, especially in linen cloth since its flax was known for its high quality. The development of long-distance maritime routes during the period 1500–1800 nevertheless greatly facilitated the diffusion of goods in the early modern period and opened new markets that could be reached for the first time. The various adaptations brought about to the kinds of textiles, mainly modest kinds of cloth, also helped to find wider markets for them.

Penetration into the world market brought with it competition from many other textile-producing centers. The most important was India: its cloth reached markets all over the world. There were also many towns within the Ottoman Empire where a lot of cloth was woven. Despite this, a number of favorable features allowed textiles from Egypt to penetrate both regional and global markets.

Diversity in the types of cloth

One reason why the demand for Egyptian cloth was high was due to the diversity of cloth produced. Textile production of Egypt was very varied. Sources mention the names of many kinds of cloth, not always easy to identify. Nevertheless, what we do know is that cloth was produced in many urban and rural areas, both in Upper Egypt and in Lower Egypt, and each one of these had its own local specialties, in the kind of cloth that was woven (silk, cotton, linen, and wool), in the weaving techniques, in the quality of cloth, and in the coloring. In Qena, in Upper Egypt, which specialized in producing cotton fabrics, one of the specialties of textile artisans was a blue striped shawl for local consumption; the blue linen cloth was woven in Asyut, while the weavers of Fayoum specialized in white woolen shawls. Mahalla, an important textile center, produced sails for ships and boats, and these were sent to Istanbul to furnish the navy. Mahalla also specialized in silk for women's wear and for household items. Its dye houses could color cloth in yellow, black, blue, orange, green, and other colors. Likewise for Dumyat (Damietta), which had an important silk production that used multiple colors for its dyes.[17]

Producing for a particular foreign clientele

A reason for the demand for these various types of textiles can be attributed to versatility on the part of the artisans, who were making particular kinds of cloth suited to specific customers, often in distant lands, adjusting the cloth to the taste of this clientele. The cloth may have been woven in a particular way or with particular materials or colors, with a specific set of clients in mind, in Africa or in Syria, for instance, and adapted to their requirements. Here, the merchants who traveled with the merchandise must have played an intermediary role between the consumers and the producers, so that the cloth was woven in such a way as to conform to the clothing needs of the consumer.

Thus, in the Upper Egyptian town of Qena, shawls were specifically produced for the African trade. In Fayoum, weavers made a kind of cloth called *kheish*, of which some twenty thousand pieces were sent every year to Syria and different countries in Europe. *Kirka* was woven in Tanta and sent to Syria via Damietta. For the caravans of the African trade going to Sinnar, weavers in Cairo made a cotton cloth dyed in red, a color much in demand in that region.[18] Going in the other direction, there was a kind of rough cloth that French merchants bought in Egypt and shipped to their Caribbean possessions to be worn by the slave population. They also purchased a kind of cloth called *foutes*, which was shipped to the port of Genoa. Ready-made clothes that were mentioned in the list of goods for which dues had been paid in the customs house of Old Cairo (Misr al-Qadima) in 1790, 1791, and 1792 include garments made of brown woolen cloth. These ready-made garments, of which some eight thousand were transported and for which customs duties were paid every year, would have had to conform to the type of clothing of the inhabitants of the locality for which they were destined.[19]

Diversity of quality, luxurious items

A further reason for the large volume of cloth that was destined for international markets was the considerable level of variety in the quality and price of the cloth. Two examples illustrate this diversity of price and quality. The first is a very luxurious and expensive type of textile—carpets; and the second is an example of a humble type of cloth of modest price. In between these two were many more kinds that are not easily identifiable. On the one hand, the carpets were evidently destined for wealthy urban populations. The so called 'Mamluk' carpets, known for their high quality and their exquisite taste, continued to be produced for some time after the end of the Mamluk state, till roughly the end of the sixteenth century and up to the seventeenth century. And as a recent publication has indicated, they were shipped to Venice, for its own consumption and as dealer for the rest of Europe.[20] In the mid-sixteenth century, these carpets were woven in the style that was highly appreciated in the Ottoman court.[21] Some of them were sent to the Imperial Palace in Istanbul and others to mosques, like the Sulimaniya in Istanbul. At the end of the seventeenth century, Vansleb refers to the export of Egyptian rugs, both the coarse kind and the fine carpets, to Marseilles. These carpets constitute one of the better known examples of luxurious cloth that was sent to various European and Ottoman destinations.

Modest cloth

On the other hand, there were kinds of cloth that were coarse, humble, ordinary, uncolored, for the consumption of modest to poor populations. One of the unacknowledged realities of this period is that large quantities of modest cloth were being exported to multiple destinations where demand was apparently very high.

Because of the shortage of studies on fabrics for the poor, the study undertaken by Colette Establet and Jean-Paul Pascual on Damascus is particularly valuable. Their book on textiles in Damascus around 1700 is based on inheritance records during the three decades going roughly from 1686 to 1717. From this study, we find out the important place that Egyptian textiles had in Damascus, in terms of both variety and quality. Among the many kinds of cloth made in Egypt, the authors noted two types in particular, referred to as *magwaz* and *baladi*, which were found in large quantities at modest prices.[22] These were ordinary humble textiles presumed to be undyed or colorless.[23] Their heavy presence in textile shops in Damascus is indicative, since it means that there was more modest cloth for sale than the higher quality cloth. We learn from André Raymond's work that the textiles that were shipped along the Red Sea to the Hijaz consisted mainly of coarse cloth.[24] This situation suggests that one cannot necessarily equate imported cloth with expensive cloth, and that in many cases, the cloth that was in demand in foreign markets was the less expensive kind.

This aspect of the textile trade is less known and less written about, even though it can reveal a lot about artisan production and the general features of the trade from 1500 to 1800. The study of this coarse cloth can also help historians to place this development in a broader context of world trade. This trend heightens the contrast with medieval trade, which was often made up of luxuries such as silks and precious stones, small in volume but high in value, as compared to early modern trade, which tended to be more bulk trade made up of ordinary goods for everyday use.

Price and quality

Finally, another incentive to purchase modest cloth was that, as observers remarked, its price was low, this being attributed to the modest cost of labor in Egypt. Also, according to observers, the cloth was more durable and flexible than similar quality cloth made elsewhere.[25] Merchants purchased very large quantities because they could make enormous profits from its sale. Many of the French purchases of cloth in Egypt consisted of this coarse kind of cloth.[26] There was an important and active export of coarse, humble, uncolored linen and cotton to a number of destinations where they were used to clothe modest to poor populations.

For these various reasons, the cloth that was made in Egypt penetrated world trade. No doubt the competition was difficult in view of the considerable production of cloth in India, but we must believe that the world market was large enough to accommodate these various producers.

The Diffusion to Four Continents

As a result of these factors, we find that the cloth made in Egypt was reaching markets in many directions. Eighteenth-century sources confirm that these exports were extensive and that the markets were multiple. Probably more than any other nonagricultural product, the cloth made in Egypt was the most important product that it exported. In the words of Monsieur de Maillet, who was for many years French consul in Cairo at the beginning of the eighteenth century, Egypt was producing "prodigious quantities" of linen cloth, which were sent to all parts of the world, and "abundant quantities" of cottons.[27] The *Description de l'Égypte*, written by the experts who accompanied Napoleon during his expedition of 1798, also provided precious information on the cloth trade and industry.

From this work, we learn a lot about textiles, where they were made, and who some of the principal consumers were. In the direction of the Hijaz, large quantities of linen were sent, and these expanded at the time of the yearly pilgrimage.[28] The African caravan carried quantities of cloth to sub-Saharan Africa. In the direction of Europe, where France was the major destination, cotton and linen textiles were sent. The list of textiles exported to France at the end of the seventeenth century given by Vansleb is impressive in its variety. It includes several kinds of cloth made in different parts of Egypt, such as the fine girdles made in Rashid (Rosetta) and linen made in Munufiya and in Alexandria. There was also blue linen; there were coarse carpets; and there were fine carpets. Vansleb also mentions little blue linen from Cairo; great blue linen from Imbaba; painted cottons; and a number of other kinds of cloth like *battanones*, *magrebines*, and *messalines*.[29] And we learn from Girard that at the end of the eighteenth century, France was purchasing from Egypt, on a yearly basis, a kind of cotton called *agami* made in Cairo; another called *mahallawi* made in Mahalla; a cloth that imitated Indian patterns; and *dimittes*, or dimity, as they were called in English, a kind of cloth known in Egypt since Fatimid times, made in Rashid.[30] Considerable amounts also went to the different parts of the Ottoman Empire—Syria, Albania, Salonica, Izmir, and of course Istanbul. In fact, most of the merchandise in the Egyptian Bazaar in Istanbul (Carsisi Misir) consisted of goods made in Egypt. A study by Sahar Khalil shows that those exported to Syria seem to have increased in the course of the eighteenth century.[31]

This very broad diffusion in different geographical directions, important as it seems, does not show the full extent of this trade. The large quantities of Egyptian cloth that French merchants purchased in Egypt, especially in the eighteenth century, much of which was of coarse quality, were in part destined for consumption in France, mostly for modest populations. But a significant portion of these textiles were re-exported to farther destinations, since French merchants were also the intermediaries who handled trade to other regions of the world, both in Europe (Holland, Spain, Italy) and in America. The cloth that was called *foutes*, which French merchants bought in Egypt and sold in the port of Genoa, was destined to be used by sailors and by the urban poor or for bedspreads.[32] The coarse Munufiya cloth *(toiles grossières)* was shipped to the French West Indies.[33] This coarse, cheaply priced cloth was one of the textiles that were intended to clothe the slave population there.[34] Another one, the *agami* cloth, was also considered to be very appropriate for slaves.[35]

In this context it is interesting to note the contrast with the cloth that was imported into the Ottoman Empire from its main European trading partner, France. While low-cost textiles from Egypt were in high demand among the different trading partners, the textiles coming to the Ottoman

Empire from France tended, on the contrary, to be of the somewhat more expensive kind. In his study of French–Ottoman trade in the eighteenth century, Edhem Eldem has noted that even though the French sent a large volume of textiles, namely the *londrins*, these were mainly for the upper- and middle-class urban population and rarely reached the lower urban strata.[36] This tells us something about both the production of textiles and the textile trade. Further research on this matter is required in order to better understand these conditions.

Impact of These Conditions on Textile Production

This wide diffusion of cloth, to the Ottoman Empire, the Hijaz, Europe, and America, inevitably had consequences on the local scene, touching various aspects in the work of artisans. One of these is an expansion of production. It did not affect all the kinds of cloth produced, but it seems to have been particularly important in relation to certain kinds, namely the coarse cloth. Generally speaking, we associate production for poor or modest populations with quantity. In other words, the quantities of cloth destined to clothe poor populations were higher than the more luxurious cloth that was to be consumed by more wealthy urban populations.

Production expands

Figures for actual production are hard to come by. The few occasional figures from the end of the eighteenth century are nevertheless indicative. Girard mentions that up to 120,000 pieces of cloth, mostly cotton, were shipped to France on a yearly basis. The figures he was referring to at the end of the eighteenth century were considerably less than those of the earlier part of the century when France was purchasing much more cloth than it did at the end of the century.[37] These figures do not take into account the other destinations which, within the Ottoman Empire, would be much higher than those shipped to France. Girard provides us with another interesting indication of the volume of cloth that was being woven. His list of the goods for which dues were paid in the customs of Old Cairo during the years 1790, 1791, and 1792 includes items that were made in very large quantities. Thus, there arrived at this customs house, on yearly average, close to 83,000 shawls from Fayoum and Upper

Egypt, and 101,622 pieces of woolen cloth were sent from Upper Egypt every year. Again, these impressively high figures do not represent the volume of cloth actually produced, but only those that were sent to Cairo and taxed at customs.[38] The three years that he referred to, from 1790 to 1792, were years of severe crisis. They witnessed conflicts between the Mamluk ruling emirs, a plague epidemic in 1791, and high food prices because of a bad Nile flood in 1792.[39] One can therefore assume that these figures represent a low point in production.

Can one talk of mass production?

Some of the developments among textile artisans and guilds were precursors of later developments—at times initiating trends that were subsequently taken up and developed in the nineteenth century, through state policies. In the case of the production of coarse cloth, one could view these conditions as being a prelude to mass production, although it would evidently be of a certain kind. Mass production is associated with the Industrial Revolution and the methods of production that accompanied it. In the present case, there was no machinery, nor was there a factory where workers were grouped in one place with the aim of producing more efficiently. How this expansion of production occured is unclear. Given the present state in research, one can only try to formulate hypotheses by comparing with other similar cases. There are examples of increased production where there is no indication or evidence that tools were improved or that factory conditions or machinery were introduced. One concept, formulated by Jan de Vries, is that of the "industrious revolution." By this, de Vries meant that in the period prior to the Industrial Revolution, there were increases in the production of market commodities that were the result of more intensive household production.[40] This could be a possible explanation. The trend was noticed in a number of countries where production increased prior to the introduction of machinery.

Another explanation could be that, in rural areas where textile production was undertaken in households by peasants in their free time, the number of part-time weavers increased as demand for cheap cloth expanded. If that were the case, then the trend toward ruralization of the textile production that John Chalcraft detected in the course of the nineteenth century would have its sources at an earlier date and for another set of reasons. The dismantling of Muhammad Ali's industries and the increased taxation on urban artisans had helped the rural textile industry to develop.[41]

Whatever was the method used to increase weaving activities, these were likely to be undertaken outside the control or surveillance of the guild. Although a lot of the weaving took place in Cairo and in other towns like Rosetta (Rashid), Mahalla al-Kubra, Alexandria, and Dumyat (Damietta), and in Qena and Asyut in Upper Egypt, some of it was also done in rural areas where numerous people who had looms in their houses worked in their spare time.[42] The expansion of the number of looms or the amount of time spent weaving was beyond the purview of any guild.

The apparently massive exports of modest cloth stand in contrast to an earlier period when high-quality Egyptian cloth was exported to Venice in the Mamluk period. The tendency that this appears to show is a move from more luxurious exports of cloth to less luxurious ones, from expensive to more commonplace. It also shows a move from a small volume of cloth to a large volume. It may have been these common stuffs, the cheap cloth woven for modest clients, that mostly attracted the attention of observers who wrote of the decline of the textile industry in Egypt. While this later trend in the expansion of modest or cheap cloth has sometimes been dismissed by scholars of art history, historians can see it from a different angle. It can be linked to a response to the market, to a significant transformation in production, and to a way of keeping up with the times.

Participating in Fashions and New Trends in Cloth

The expansion in the production of cheap cloth was one of the consequences of world trade on the local scene. It was, however, not the only one. Other consequences for the local making of cloth were likewise the result of world trading conditions. This time it was manifested in the production of cotton cloth with Indian designs. This Indian-style cloth can be associated with an urban population, more or less prosperous, in contrast with the coarse undyed cloth for modest populations, traced above. Unlike available sources regarding the production of modest cloth, which leave us with a number of unanswered questions about which we can only hypothesize, the court archives—the sources regarding the printed cottons with Indian designs in demand worldwide—provide us with information that helps us address a number of issues. The impact of this new trend is apparent in urban guilds. New guilds specializing in this kind of cloth were created. In addition to this, innovative ways of structuring guilds made their appearance, as entrepreneurial methods made their way to the fore.

The expansion in cotton cloth in the eighteenth century

As of the seventeenth century, there was an unprecedented popularity of Indian-style cotton textiles worldwide, which made this item very much in demand among a certain class of the urban population. This fashion for Indian-style cotton prints—whether those made in India or those made in numerous other textile-producing centers that followed the same inspiration and imitated the Indian designs—became what Giorgio Riello and Prasannan Parthasarathi called a "global commodity." By the eighteenth century, these cottons were sold not only in Europe and the Middle East, but all over Asia, as well as Japan, Africa, and America.[43]

There were various echoes of this trend in Egypt. Firstly, it appears that more and more cotton was being planted in Egypt—its agriculture undergoing an expansion in the eighteenth century—a necessary prerequisite for any expansion in the production of cotton cloth. Second, in Cairo, as in numerous cities of the empire, in their attempts to keep up with this growing market, artisans were weaving larger quantities of cotton cloth, in keeping with the demand, both locally and internationally.[44] Third, the amount of cloth that Egypt was exporting was also on the increase. Raymond's studies of commercial relations between France and Egypt clearly illustrate this trend. Of all textiles that Egypt exported to Europe in the eighteenth century, nine-tenths went to France; and of the large amounts of cloth that France was purchasing in Egypt, he notes the following unexpected figures: two-thirds of its purchases were for cotton cloth and one-third for linen cloth—unexpected because Egypt was a great producer of linen and its linen had been a standard product for many centuries.[45] The expansion of cotton, from its planting to its weaving to its trade, was a reflection of the commercial conditions of the time.

Creating new guilds in Cairo

In the latter part of the seventeenth and in the eighteenth century, as the demand for Indian-style cloth intensified, a number of textile guilds in Cairo were formed specializing in cloth of Indian inspiration, commonly known in France as *indiennes*. This occured at a time when the market for Indian cloth and Indian designs had spread to many parts of the world, including the Ottoman Empire and Europe. Numerous textile centers were trying to imitate these kinds of cloth—in Damascus, Diyarbakr, Istanbul, and Marseilles, to mention a few.

In 1121/1709, for example, there is a reference to a guild that specialized in dyeing Indian cotton. Presumably the members of this guild had an agreement with the makers of plain cotton cloth and they dyed this cloth in designs that were similar to those of Indian textiles.[46] Another guild, which was made up of nine dyers of "cotton cloth dyed in the style of India and Diyarbakr," is mentioned in 1082/1671.[47] The artisans who were part of this guild, mentioned by name, included two Armenians, two Christians from Aleppo, and one artisan from Diyarbakr in eastern Anatolia. In other words, these artisans had come to Cairo with certain skills (the style of Diyarbakr) that they were introducing to Cairo. Why Diyarbakr, a town in western Anatolia, very far from Cairo? In all probability, because in Diyarbakr, textile workers were manufacturing a kind of cloth called *ja'farani*, which had beautiful Indian designs in bright colors and very finely designed, of apparently superior quality.[48] The Diyarbakr cottons were in vogue in France as well, and imported to Marseilles where in the seventeenth century local artisans tried to imitate them.[49]

Bringing new adjustments to older crafts

Court archives of Cairo indicate that textile guilds were expanding in cloth decorated in the technique called *basma*. Printed textiles, so fashionable in the eighteenth century, were not new to Egypt. Art historians have long known that during the Mamluk period (1250–1517) printed textiles were produced, and a number of examples were found in recent excavations. These too were influenced by Indian designs. There was, however, a difference in the area of coloring between the Mamluk block prints and those produced in the eighteenth century. Mamluk printed cloth primarily made use of indigo for its color, indigo being locally produced and relatively available.[50] In the late period, the emphasis was on color, and this is presumably what distinguished the earlier prints from the later ones. In 1780 the guild of printers on textiles *(basmajiya)* specialized in making designs of an Indian style.[51] In this guild, some of the artisans came from Istanbul, Bosnia, Diyarbakr, and Syria.

Initiating new fashions

One final example of the way that guilds in Cairo integrated the growing world demand for Indian cloth and expanded their production of works in this style is in Kashmir shawls. A guild of dyers was formed in Cairo whose specialization was to take old Kashmir shawls imported from India and to re-dye them with multiple colors so as to make them look new. When the Napoleonic Expedition arrived in Egypt, and its experts recorded the various activities of the inhabitants, a list of guilds was made, and this particular guild was included under the name "raccommodeurs de châles Kashmir au Caire." These dyers were also mentioned by Jomard, who wrote about them saying that the dyers of Cairo were extremely agile in the way they took old shawls and made them look new and fresh. They dyed them in red, yellow, skin color, and dark colors. He warned French visitors that it was very easy to mistake them for original Indian ones; they were so well made that sometimes they surpassed the original, except that the price was much lower.[52] Following the Napoleonic Expedition to Egypt, by the nineteenth century, Kashmir shawls became extremely popular in France after the officers of the Napoleonic Expedition took a sample with them on their return from Egypt, so much so that when Napoleon married Marie-Louise, he gave her a gift of seventeen Kashmir shawls.[53]

The complex colored designs of the Kashmir shawls mentioned by Jomard seem to have required a sophisticated dyeing technique. The complexities of this technique are well illustrated by the fact that when French dyers, following the Napoleonic Expedition, took these Kashmir shawls to France and tried to imitate them, they failed miserably. They found it impossible to combine such a large number of colors interlaced with each other. It took years of experimentation before they could get the colors right.[54] They were then imitated in Scotland, in Paisley, a town that gave its name to the designs on this kind of shawl. Prior to that, they were being imitated in Persia. Hence, one can place the guild in Cairo, which was dyeing these Kashmir circles in the context of a broader trend that was followed in many different and faraway regions.

Diffusion of Trends by Merchants and by Artisans

Merchants had an intermediary role between producer and consumer when it came to diffusing information from one place to another. A considerable portion of the Indian textiles sent to the various parts of the Ottoman Empire and Europe passed through their hands as items of the Red Sea trade, which they controlled. All the major merchants of the eighteenth century dealt extensively in Indian textiles and made enormous fortunes by importing Indian textiles and shipping them to farther destinations. The networks that they operated were primarily to handle goods, but in doing so, they also spread information, on, for instance, new trends and fashions. This gave them the potential to be a link to the consumer in a distant land from the local producer. These networks that merchants maintained can in part help to explain how a number of textile-producing towns of the Ottoman Empire—Istanbul, Cairo, Aleppo, Urfa, Ayntab (Gaziantep), Diyarbakr—were all weaving cloth with designs that imitated the ones coming from India.

Artisan transfers

What is more unexpected is to see that during the seventeenth and eighteenth centuries, there seems to have been a pattern for artisans who were highly specialized to move from one region to another, carrying their skills with them. This trend has been observed in different parts of the Ottoman Empire, not only in Cairo. Istanbul too formed a pole of attraction for artisans from other regions—Persians fleeing from the troubles in their country, Indians who came with their expertise in textiles, East Asians who settled there and worked as artisans, Greeks from Chios who had learned to imitate the cloth that came from Italy, and Armenians.[55] On the whole, Egypt seems to have been on the receiving end. Examples of Egyptian artisans moving to other regions are uncommon. There is a reference to an artisan transfer from Egypt to Europe, namely a carpet weaver who was brought to Venice to weave carpets in the Mamluk style, of which one example survives.[56] In the late sixteenth century, in 1585, the Ottoman sultan Murad III summoned eleven carpet weavers to come to Istanbul from Cairo with their materials. Again, this example is not typical of that period insofar as it was a state order rather than a voluntary move.

The presence of these outsiders in the cloth-making domain is interesting for a number of reasons. The ease with which foreign craftsmen were integrated is a reflection of an expansion in production. It meant that there was a place for these incoming artisans in the guild: otherwise their presence would have been resisted. Their presence also indicates a certain openness of these guilds, given what we know about the restrictions that some guilds imposed on newcomers. When craftsmen were concerned about competition, they tended to limit the number of people who could practice their craft. We see this in a court case dating from the early decades of the eighteenth century. The craftsmen who made yogurt asked the qadi to confirm their guild rules, which specified that no one was to become a guild member except the children or family members of present guild members.[57] The objective was to limit entrance to the guild and to try to maintain a stable number of members. The qadi complied, the basis for his decision being the guild rules. The contrast between guilds such as these and those working in cloth highlights the direction in which textile guilds were developing.

These moves by artisans within the circle comprising the Ottoman, Mughal, and Safavid states had their parallels in other regions. As new technologies were developed and competition for markets increased, this kind of artisan transfer seems to have become fairly commonly practiced in early modern Europe. David Landes has shown that about two thousand British skilled workers were transferred to the continent in order to show workmen there how to use new techniques, even though there was a prohibition by the British government against doing so.[58] Artisans were transferred from England to France in 1718 to teach French factory workers in Paris and Normandy watchmaking and metalworking.[59]

Consequences of these moves, circulation of know-how

This aspect of artisans' lives has not been explored to any extent. Possibly the numbers involved were not very large, although estimates are almost impossible to make. Nevertheless, as a phenomenon, transfers of this kind, even if limited, had their significance. They had the potential to help in the circulation of techniques and methods of work among artisans. And whatever techniques and methods were transferred were also adapted to a different environment by men with different skills. At the same time, these transfers created a certain degree of similarity between the product that was made in one city and another. At this stage, there was still a high level of local diversity between the products of different regions, but one can nevertheless see the beginnings of a greater level of standardization of tastes that would become more apparent with time.

One last point about these transfers is that they were early examples of the better-known transfers of artisans and technicians that took place in the nineteenth century under Muhammad Ali. These much-written-about foreign artisans came to Egypt to work in the newly established factories and in the printing press. But little attention has been paid to the precedents in Egypt of these artisan transfers. Muhammad Ali was in fact continuing—possibly on a larger scale—to do what artisans had been doing on their own initiative for some time.

These exchanges created links between the various textile-producing centers in the Ottoman Empire where artisans were using similar techniques and similar fashions of cloth production. They also created links between the Ottoman Empire, Persia, and India, which was the inspiration of many of the innovations in textiles. Thus, cloth created a level of connection between these three empires that are not often studied in relation to economic history. Because a lot of the focus has been on trade and commerce—the Mediterranean or the Red Sea trade—little has been written about possible connections among artisans in Egypt, India, or Persia. We can now add to what we know about the role of merchants in circulating knowledge of textile artisans. These contacts and mutual influences seem to have been a feature characteristic of the early modern period that even the artisans of Egypt, who probably did not travel much, felt. One effective term to describe these parallelisms is what Joseph Fletcher called "horizontal continuities" between societies that were geographically far apart.[60]

In addition to the circulation that linked Ottoman with Persian and Indian, one could add to this another circle, that of France, which in the seventeenth century became interested in producing what became known in France as *indiennes*, or cloth decorated in the style of Indian textiles. In Avignon, Languedoc, and Marseilles, these imitations started to appear. Here too the expertise of Ottoman artisans was used. [61] As Giorgio Riello states, the French *indiennes* were a copy of the Ottoman *indiennes*, which were a copy of the Indian ones.[62] Textile production, in other words, was connecting these cities to one another.

Internal Adjustments in Guilds

The various kinds of innovations in textile production in seventeenth- and eighteenth-century Cairo are indications that textile guilds developed along a somewhat different path from many other guilds, and that they were often not in conformity with the practices usually associated with guilds. Many of the innovations that were undertaken, in creating new guilds, incorporating new techniques, or expanding their production, implicitly show that guild practice had to be adapted or adjusted to incorporate these initiatives. There were several ways in which these changes were taking place.

Islamic law versus guild law

One of these was in the domain of courts and qadis. The courts, generally speaking, were resorted to by guilds in order to confirm their choice of guild head, or in order to confirm the rules agreed to by the members of the guild, referred to as *qanun*. A large number of guild rules were, strictly speaking, not in accordance with Islamic law. For instance, Islamic law prohibited monopoly; it did not look favorably on restrictions that guilds often imposed on members, such as not allowing them to work in two crafts or not allowing persons outside a guild to pursue the craft undertaken by that guild. These were intended to protect members from unfair competition. When a court case regarding these guild rules was presented to the qadi, he normally confirmed guild regulations on the basis of their being the *qanun* of the guild or its customary practice.

Although by and large this continued to be the case in the eighteenth century, we nevertheless find, in a few cases, a different approach from qadis; they go against guild rules and apply Islamic law, which tended to be more liberal. Often these unusual cases were connected to textile artisans and guilds. One instance is of a workshop in the town of al-Mahalla al-Kubra, in which, in 1120/1708, the head of the guild of tassel-makers *('aqqadin)* and its members complained to the qadi about a merchant who employed tassel-makers, weavers *(hayyakin)*, and tailors in his workshop, presumably in order to make ready-made clothes; it was against the rules to employ workers from different crafts. Normally, the qadi would have upheld the rules of the guild. However, this time his decision took another direction. He ruled that as long as the artisans did their work well, there was no reason to stop them from practicing.[63]

A year later in Cairo, 1121/1709, a similar case came to the attention of the qadi. This time the guild of dyers of Indian cotton filed a complaint against a person who was practicing two crafts, that of a dyer of Indian cotton, and that of a printer on cotton *(basmaji)*. The guild had taken a decision that its members could not undertake two crafts. Taking an unusual decision, the qadi went against the guild and decided that its rules did not conform to the sharia; a guild, he decided, could not stop anyone from practicing a craft.[64]

In these and other similar decisions, the qadi's decision was in keeping with a more liberal approach to production, one that was not hampered by as many rules as guilds tended to follow. Even though this kind of decision was not the rule, it nevertheless is an indication of a change taking place, albeit on a limited scale. One can link it to a context—namely, it was in keeping with the importance of the cloth production industry in Egypt.

How did these conditions change work organization?

One can also discern some changes in the work organization related to artisans. Traditionally, textile artisans worked in small workshops that had a few looms, four or five or a few more, for the most part owned by an artisan. He either sold his cloth directly to a client or to a merchant. What happens in the eighteenth century, when we know that the volume of textiles exported to other countries underwent a significant increase, is a change not of tools or equipment but of organization. The court records indicate a number of methods that were used in organizing work that potentially led to more rationalized and efficient production.

These methods were varied and did not conform to one single pattern. For instance, the work of Naser Uthman on eighteenth-century Rashid, an important textile-producing town, shows that entrepreneurs—merchants or notables—had an upper hand in organizing the production of textile artisans, and although most workshops were owned by artisans themselves, these entrepreneurs emerged as owners of textile-producing workshops. A weaver by the name of Hajj Hijazi ibn Salim "Ibn Tarikha," for example, owned five weaving workshops, two yarn workshops, and one dye house. Thus, several stages in the production of textiles were under his control, a method that helped improve efficiency in the production. Likewise a notable, Hajj Muhammad Zaqzuq, owned five weaving workshops and one workshop for bleaching yarn. Another such entrepreneur in eighteenth-century Rashid was Muhammad Muhammad, a merchant and the head of the Maghribi community of Alexandria, who owned two linen-weaving workshops and one cotton-weaving workshop.[65]

In the town of Mahalla, a major textile center, Husam Abdul-Mu'ti's work shows another method by which an entrepreneur controlled a small textile business—a merchant who ran an enterprise which was obviously larger than the usual simple weaving workshop with a few looms. He was employing artisans who specialized in weaving, in tassel-making, and in tailoring clothes, all working under his supervision. Presumably his objective was to produce ready-made garments for the market. This enterprise was unusual insofar as it employed a number of people undertaking different crafts; it had several stages in the production of the finished garments; the owner, being himself a merchant, would also handle the commercial distribution of the garments.[66]

Still another form of a textile business was undertaken by the guild of printers on cloth *(basmajiya)* in Cairo in 1194/1780, by which the guild members decided that they should all work in one location and that the profits of their work should be divided among the members in set proportions: the guild shaykh and fourteen other members would each get one part of the profit. This organization of work—quite unlike the traditional craft production that was based on a person's work and output—meant that they could produce their printed textiles more efficiently. It might also be a way to check uniformity or quality of production. This agreement was a long-term arrangement, probably aimed at reaching a broad market.[67]

What these various examples show is the variety of arrangements that were undertaken to face the prevailing situation, some by the artisans themselves, and others by entrepreneurs.

Conclusions

Conditions of the seventeenth and eighteenth centuries brought textile artisans to the vanguard of change in relation to other producers. These changes touched on their links to the world economy as well as on their internal organization in their guilds and in their practice. They produced more; they adapted production to the needs of the market. This meant that some of the cloth was in line with world fashions for printed cottons, Indian style. It also meant producing a large amount of cheap cloth destined for poor or modest populations, including the slaves working in the French West Indies.

Adapting to the world market led to growing similarities between the work of artisans in Cairo and those in other textile centers of the Mediterranean and Ottoman worlds and beyond. Many cities in the Ottoman Empire and in Europe—Cairo, Marseilles, and Istanbul, among others—were producing the same kind of cloth that imitated Indian designs. Thus, a growing connectedness was emerging between regions that were relatively far apart, and textile production was one of the factors that contributed to it.

Adapting to the growing commercial demands on local cloth also meant that changes were introduced in the guild, working methods, and work organization. These changes, nevertheless, did not touch all aspects of the guild or the lives and work of the artisans. In many other ways, their practices continued to conform to traditional norms: the hierarchical position of the guild head in the structure and the obedience owed him by members were among the features that seem to have had continuity, even with textile guilds that had taken a different path. Thus, these guilds combined both aspects, an international dimension that linked to developments associated with the world economy and a traditional aspect linked to their own past as guild members who cherished their traditions of solidarity and loyalty, a hybrid situation that combined local and global.

In all these features, artisans and guilds involved in cloth-making were developing along a certain path, and this path was different from that of many other mainstream guilds that had a limited sphere of activity, in terms of both its geographical sphere of practice and its markets. Thus one can place them in relation to these features at the vanguard of change.

The developments in the seventeenth and eighteenth centuries shed light on a little-known period in the history of textiles in Egypt. Few textiles of this period can be found in museums, compared to examples of Mamluk textiles. On the whole they have not been studied by historians or art historians. Nevertheless, the often-repeated idea that the textile production of Egypt declined after the Mamluk period (1250–1517) is put into question here.[68] Textile production continued to be very active, textiles were in demand in many international markets, and, finally, there were innovations taking place in the way textiles were produced. These developments push us to reconsider much of what has been written about the decline of textiles after the Mamluk period. The Ottoman period in Egypt has been associated with the decline of the textile industry, which had flourished in the past.

The findings of this chapter do not fit the theme of a decline of textiles. One reason for the difference in view is that, in general, the study of textiles as history, rather than as art history, provides one with a different perspective about its importance both to the economy and to subsequent developments. Art historians of medieval Islamic textiles consider that the production of textiles in Egypt underwent a serious decline in the late medieval period. For instance, Louise Mackie states that during the fourteenth century, the Mamluk textile industry flourished and was a dominant force in textile commerce throughout the Mediterranean and in the east–west spice trade. She finds that the decline of quality and the rise in prices of fifteenth-century textiles contributed to the economic depression of the fifteenth century. In the meantime, the innovations in textile technology in Europe enabled finer and cheaper textiles to flood the Mamluk market.[69] At this point, Egypt could no longer compete in the textile market. This view should be reconsidered in the light of the new material that is emerging on this subject.

Egypt has a long history in its textile industry. Textiles were produced during pharaonic times, Coptic textiles are well known for their peculiar designs, textile production continued in the early Islamic period and reached new heights under Fatimid rulers, and high-quality textiles were produced under the Mamluk state. Each period had its specificities and developed its techniques. The seventeenth and eighteenth centuries show innovations not only in the techniques of production, such as the dyes or the decorations on the cloth, but also in the expansion of the production of cheap coarse cloth which was in tremendous demand in the international market due to its price and its durability. The vitality of the cloth industry must be sought in other aspects of its production that remain to be explored. It is, consequently, important to identify the criterion that is appropriate to that particular period when comparisons are made with earlier periods.

The local, regional, and international conditions of this crucial period were such that textile guilds, by the nature of their product and their markets and the technical adjustments that artisans made, were brought closer to subsequent developments, namely with the industrialization policy in textile production introduced by Muhammad Ali in the early decades of the nineteenth century. He too aimed at selling this product in the world market. The study of textile guilds in the seventeenth and eighteenth centuries thus shows some of the antecedents of Muhammad Ali's policies. It indicates that there were eighteenth-century sources for some of the developments taking place in the first half of the nineteenth century. But there were also differences. In the eighteenth century, the initiatives did not come from state policies, but many of them emerged as a result of the initiatives of artisans and guilds. In the nineteenth century, it was state policy, rather than small artisans and producers, that shaped the direction of the developments that would bring Egypt much closer to the world economy.

A last point of textile history takes us to the beginning of the nineteenth century and Muhammad Ali's industrial policy. If we place this policy in relation to the previous period, the eighteenth century, for instance, this requires us to reconsider a few points. In a general way, Muhammad Ali was given credit for his innovative industrial policy. In reality, some of the ground had already been prepared for the accomplishment of his policy. But he deserves some credit, notably for having realized that there was a basis for his decision to emphasize textiles in his policy of industrialization: this basis consisted of the presence of skilled artisans; the existence of markets for local textiles; some of the innovative practices initiated by artisans and their guilds that had already been current; and the idea that it was best to make use of existing facilities in order to start a new industry. It was not only the impetus coming from Europe that pushed him to choose textiles, but the realization that there were also local foundations upon which to build his initiatives.

4 Artisans, Spies, and Manufacturers: Eighteenth-century Transfers of Technology from the Ottoman Empire to France

Transfer of Know-how, Alternatives to Eurocentrism

The nineteenth century witnessed a transfer of science and technology from Europe to other parts of the world. The introduction of railways, steamships, banks, telegraphs, hotels and tourist companies, numerous tools and machines—all these innovations changed the face of many cities in the non-European world. Coming at a time of growing European control of various parts of the world, these transfers were accompanied by a hegemonic discourse on the benefits that science and technology, with the material progress that accompanied them, could bring to 'backward' societies. They were associated with the 'civilizing role' of colonialism, the main agency in spreading science and technology from the scientific core to the non-scientific periphery. The transfers of technology were thus represented as the positive side of colonialism.[1]

Current perceptions promoted the image of the world outside Europe as 'backward' regions. There was nevertheless a distinction that was made in favor of regions like Egypt or India, which, in prior periods, had had high levels of civilization; these were perceived as having declined from their earlier glory some time before the early modern period. They were compared to regions that did not in their past history have high levels of civilization like those of Egypt or India, for the most part in Africa and America. These regions were seen as being primitive or barbarian. In either case, regions outside Europe had simple or primitive technologies and their inhabitants had poor or no skills. They consequently had little to offer the more sophisticated men of science in the developed world, except perhaps abundant quality raw material, which could be put to better use in Europe. Consequently this up-to-down discourse dismissed the possibility of a transfer occurring in the other direction—that is, from east to west—or of transfers from down to up, and from craftsmen and artisans to modern science or industry. The transfer of knowledge was a one-way affair and its direction was from Europe to the rest of the world.

These views both had a significant influence on, and were supported by, historical studies. Histories of Asia, India, or the Middle East were in part inspired by the hegemonic discourse of the nineteenth century. The theme of dynamic European inventiveness, with Europe as giver, as opposed to the static recipients of knowledge, was a theme that was applied to numerous societies, including the Middle East. But studies have indicated that during the medieval period, Islamic sciences had developed considerably and had an impact on European sciences. The works of Roshdi Rashed and George Saliba have shown this clearly.[2] Many of the mainstream histories of science nevertheless still perceive Greece to have been the only source for the development of European sciences and, in spite of these studies, Islamic sciences have not found their place in the standard chronology. For the most part, histories of science consider that the development of Islamic sciences was arrested after the medieval period, or the Golden Age of Islam. One explanation for their decline was their failure to give birth to modern science, an argument that appears to be circular.[3] Arabs consequently became recipients of knowledge from the west. Another explanation for the decline of Arab sciences, propounded by one of the greatest proponents of European superiority, was that Islamic culture considered that scientific or philosophical speculation would divert the believers from attention to God.[4] Such cultural explanations for European superiority and supposed non-European backwardness imply a certain level of determinism, and of the impossibility for so-called 'backward' cultures to change for the better.

Thus, the history of science in the modern period was written as a history of European science and technology and its impact on other regions of the world outside Europe.[5] A good example, written fairly recently, can be found in volume four of the *Cambridge History of Science*, which deals with the eighteenth century. The chapter on "Islam" refers several times to sciences in the Islamic world as conservative or traditional. It deplores the fact that European sciences did not have a great impact on the Islamic world, and notes, with regard to medicine, a considerable delay between European development and its transmission to the Middle East. Thus, its emphasis is on the impact of European science on the Islamic world, showing, for instance, how European medicine influenced physicians in Istanbul.[6] Few historians have so far taken an interest in scientific activity that took place in the Islamic world of the later period. Among these one should cite William Gervase Clarence-Smith's short survey of the sciences in the early modern Islamic world;[7] and more specifically about Egypt, Peter Gran, Sabri al-Adl, and Raimer Broemer's studies of eighteenth-century Cairo.[8] These studies are yet to be taken from the restricted domain of area studies and placed in a broader context of world history.

Revisionist Views about the Transfer of Know-how

In the past few years, however, a number of revisionist scholars, at both the theoretical and the empirical levels, have challenged the dominant paradigm, implying that knowledge was not a one-way process, that it did not originate in any one single region, but rather that it had numerous sources and circulated in different directions.[9] One of these, James Blaut, argued against what he called the "diffusionist" model of history, which upheld the idea that there was one single center from which knowledge was diffused to the rest of the world, and that center was Europe, while the rest of the world was the recipient of European knowledge. He, on the contrary, claimed that the making of "modern Europe" was in part forged by the non-European world.[10]

A number of empirical studies have followed a similar line, focusing on India, Asia, and the Americas from the sixteenth century onward, and providing concrete examples of the way that local knowledge of American Indians, Southeast Asians, and Indians was taken over by Europeans and integrated into European sciences. The French scholar Bertrand Romain, for example, perceives the "great discoveries" of the sixteenth century not solely as a result of the effort of European visionaries but as their combined efforts with the inhabitants of Southeast Asia; for him, the developments in European science and technology of the period owe a debt to the auxiliary sources of local informers and local knowledge. The Dutch who arrived in Sumatra in the closing year of the sixteenth century knew none of the local languages and could only communicate through local interpreters. They likewise had to rely on locals to provide them with information on how and where to navigate and ultimately on how to draw maps of the region.[11] The maps that were ultimately drawn were fully attributed to the Dutch as if they had been done solely by them. In reality they would not have been able to draw them had they not had the help of numerous local persons. The historian Andrés Pireto found the same to be true in Spanish South America. The discoveries of the Jesuit priests there were based on the local knowledge that they had acquired from the natives, and this knowledge ultimately contributed to the development of sixteenth- and seventeenth-century science. Traditional healing methods were found to cure diseases which academic medicine was unable to handle. The medicinal plants and 'traditional knowledge' that the natives used as cures were sometimes at the source of pharmaceutical products. In the process, this knowledge was appropriated by the Spanish, and the role of the native was effaced.[12] The emphasis of this approach is that the technical knowledge that ultimately came to be one of the bases of the modern world was formulated by both parties, the colonizer and the colonized.

Scholarship on this subject has focused on Asia, India, and America. The study of contributions of Ottoman lands in general, or of Egypt in particular, both of which had considerable commercial exchanges with Europe in the early modern period, are still in an early stage and need to be explored much more fully, as studies on this subject are still few.[13]

Taking off from this standpoint, the purpose of the present study is first to look at transfers of know-how and technology from the Ottoman Empire (with an emphasis on Egypt) to Europe, with a special focus on France, because it was the main trading partner of the Ottoman Empire in the seventeenth and eighteenth centuries; many of the transfers to France were eventually diffused from there to other parts of Europe.

The study of south–north exchanges, rather than the other way around, is relevant both for its own sake and for a broader understanding of relations between south and north. The central issue of this exploration is the attempt to understand the contributions of non-European knowledge to the formation of the modern world.

A second purpose of the present study is to examine the relationship between scholars and artisans to find out whether artisans had a contribution to make in the development of modern science and technology. Can these exchanges be seen as a down-to-up process? Of such artisan/scholar exchanges taking place in Egypt we know little, other than what the historian al-Jabarti writes about his father, Shaykh Hasan al-Jabarti, to whom he devotes a lengthy obituary (d. 1188/1774). Hasan al-Jabarti, a man of many talents, well versed in Islamic sciences, had a special interest in astronomy and geometry. To this end he gathered in his house numerous artisans and craftsmen who explained to him how to make astrolabes, quandrants, and geometrical instruments.[14] Al-Jabarti was evidently trying to combine his theoretical knowledge with the practical know-how of the local craftsmen.

The contribution of local artisans and crafts knowledge in the creation of modern science has for long been a subject of debate. This debate revolves around the following question: What was the scientific value of knowledge gained, neither through an intellectual or philosophical process, nor in a scientific laboratory, but rather by persons who were not necessarily literate, like the artisans or craftsmen who obtained their knowledge from their daily practice, from trial and error, and whose knowledge was based on material objects rather than on texts? If scientific knowledge had a universal quality, did the concrete, localized forms of knowledge have an equal value? The question that this raises is what, if any, was the role of artisan know-how in the creation of modern science. This debate has particular relevance in view of the extensive exchanges taking place in the early modern period. Recent scholarship on the subject of the seventeenth century proposes to reconsider the textbook explanation that attributes the Scientific Revolution to important European thinkers like Bacon, Copernicus, Newton, Descartes, and Galileo, suggesting that the contribution of innumerable anonymous artisans should also be included.[15] This represents an important advance in scholarship on this subject. However, most of the literature that questions the mainstream narrative on the Scientific Revolution has focused on the contributions of European artisans to various scientific fields.

The present chapter contributes to this discussion by an examination of non-European artisans with the objective of finding out where this trend can be placed in relation to the debate.

Emerging Interest in Crafts

This period of the long eighteenth century was crucial with regard to relations between the Ottoman Empire and Europe. It was a period prior to the nineteenth-century European domination of the Middle East and the creation of dependent economies. At the same time, it was a period during which commercial relations between the Ottoman world and Europe were very active, presumably more intense than before. Together with this intensive commercial activity, another kind of exchange was also taking place—exchange of know-how, information, and knowledge. During the eighteenth century, French entrepreneurs and producers were interested in finding out about the know-how and technologies of the Ottoman Empire because this was a period of inventions and progress, and one in which the Industrial Revolution was starting to emerge. There were many channels. Merchants, spies, manufacturers, priests, consuls, scientists, and chemists, among others, traveled in different parts of the Ottoman Empire as well as to other parts of the world. Often they were sponsored by the state; often too they were sponsored by royal academies. The Jesuit missionaries who came to Egypt, like those who traveled to many other parts of the world, were also involved in the collection of information. Often they had a head start over others due to their long residence in the country and their familiarity with the language. They, like others, observed the way things were done, and the information they collected was sent back home. Globally, this information, much of which is published, now forms an excellent source on the subject of transfers for scholars and historians.

The various travelers coming to the Ottoman Empire in the eighteenth century described numerous craft techniques which impressed them and which they subsequently imitated when they returned to their country. I need mention here only a few. One of these is a flour mill that a French traveler, Jean-Claude Flachat, who was in Constantinople in the 1760s, found to be so efficient that he built a similar one in his hometown of Lyon.[16] There were also a number of medical cures that the French found in Egypt, learned from local physicians, especially at the time of the Napoleonic Expedition (1798–1801); then they used these in their own hospitals once they returned to France. One of these was a cure for an eye ailment, ophthalmia. Ophthalmia was an endemic disease in Egypt.[17] This ailment, unknown to Europeans till the Napoleonic Expedition, hit the French troops hard, and many soldiers were blinded. Subsequently the French troops left Egypt, taking the disease with them, and soon afterward it attacked the British army, infecting its troops; many of them too were blinded. As the French troops subsequently moved from place to place, they brought the disease to the countries they went to in Europe, especially as the Napoleonic armies advanced toward new lands, infecting both civilian and military populations. Ophthalmia had become a European disease at a time when European doctors knew little about it. The French army doctors had tried several remedies on the soldiers who had caught this infection, but the most successful was the one local doctors were using.[18] The remedies that Egyptian oculists practiced were subsequently implemented when the disease spread in epidemic form in 1832 in an orphanage (Maison de Refuge) in Paris, and they met with success.[19] These and many other remedies commonly practiced in Egypt were eventually incorporated into the domains of academic medicine, and they were implemented in European treatment of these diseases. According to Catherine Kelly, the encounters of French and British medical officers in Egypt not only influenced their practice in later military campaigns but also fostered the idea among military practitioners that military medicine required specialized knowledge.[20]

These are some of many examples of a local craft becoming integrated into a universal science. There are others that are still in need of exploration. They push us to raise questions about the relationship of science and technology to the know-how of artisans. Often, artisan know-how and scientific knowledge are considered as distinct domains, science dealing with intellectual matters and technology with the more practical and concrete. This classification implies a hierarchy, with science being given an elevated position and technology a lesser one. But the practical know-how of artisans played an important role, one that has been undervalued, in the development of the modern world. The cure for ophthalmia provides a good example of the efficiency of a 'traditional' medical treatment, and boosts the argument that the distinction made between practical know-how and theoretical knowledge is not always as clear-cut as is often implied. These are issues that one would need to rethink in the context of the early modern world.

France and the Ottoman Empire: Textile Technology

Of the many other examples of transfers of know-how, there is one item that seems to have attracted more attention of French entrepreneurs and merchants—the domain of textile technology. French sources of the eighteenth and early nineteenth centuries show a great interest in the attempts at learning the know-how of artisans in Cairo, Edirne, and Istanbul in the production of textiles. It is through French sources that we can find out what in particular they were looking for, how the techniques and know-how were transmitted or transferred, who was involved in the transfer, and in some cases, what became of them once they reached France, and how some of them penetrated into the French textile industry.

The present study will focus on the transfer of textile technology to France, and on the search of French producers, entrepreneurs, and academic societies for new methods that improved textile production in the Ottoman Empire. The focus on textiles is significant because although European travelers who went to the east were often in search of the exotic and the unusual, for items like strange animals or mysterious monsters, in the present case we are dealing with down-to-earth, immediate economic interests.

The importance of textiles was multiple

The importance of textile production in the eighteenth century was multiple. Firstly, as the Industrial Revolution was emerging, textile trade and production was at the heart of industrial production and of growing economies. For many European nations, therefore, it was important to improve their industries, of which the textile industry was not only the most important but also the motor behind the Industrial Revolution. It is not surprising that, more than anything else, French sources on the subject show a great interest in finding out about techniques linked to textiles that could be useful to their own manufactures.

In many regions, it was through textiles that Europeans extended their economic hegemony. One well-known instance took place in the nineteenth century, in the form of British control over Egypt, closely linked to its need for Egyptian cotton for its textile industries. Consequently, the eighteenth century witnessed a high level of competition over markets, involving the different textile-producing centers in the Ottoman Empire, in European countries such as France and England, and of course between the Ottoman world and Europe. The search for new processes that could help competition in terms of price or quality were certainly not limited to Egypt or to the Ottoman Empire, since France and England were also seriously competing against each other. It is in this context that we can place the search for new techniques and methods of production. The French, in their search for new techniques, were in fact trying to outstrip the English.

The textile industry was of considerable economic weight both in Europe and in the Ottoman Empire. Not only were there numerous important textile-producing centers in the Ottoman Empire, such as Istanbul, Bursa, Edirne, Diyarbakr, Aleppo, Damascus, and Cairo, but textiles were also the major product of exchange between the Ottomans and India as well as between them and France in the eighteenth century. In Egypt, the textile industry had a history that went back for many centuries, during which artisans had accumulated a large body of inherited know-how. In the course of the eighteenth century, it had adopted new fashions and techniques to keep up with the demands of the world market, expanding its production of cotton cloth and forming new guilds to answer demand for cloth with Indian patterns and designs.[21] With time, as the fashion for these Indian-style cotton textiles grew, attempts were made in many textile centers in the Ottoman Empire to produce textiles similar to these or using the same patterns. In many cities in the Ottoman Empire, new guilds specialized in printing colored designs on

Indian cotton emerged in the mid-seventeenth and eighteenth centuries.[22] This trend was observed in Cairo, Syria, and Anatolia.

Throughout the eighteenth century, France purchased enormous amounts of cloth made in the Ottoman Empire—from Istanbul, Izmir, Bilad al-Sham, and Egypt. France was the main distributor of Ottoman merchandise in Europe, having replaced Venice since the beginning of the seventeenth century. From the port of Marseilles, where the Ottoman merchandise was shipped, it was redistributed to a number of other destinations. At the same time, in an attempt to encourage local textile production, the French authorities made numerous attempts to limit these imports of cloth from the Levant and to try to manufacture them locally. French mercantile policy was, to a considerable extent, a motor behind the attempts to imitate oriental goods rather than to import them.

To this purpose, the search by French producers for new methods in textile production took them to various parts of the world. Factory owners, merchants, and entrepreneurs traveled to faraway places outside Europe searching for new methods to improve their textile production. For some Frenchmen, this search took them all the way to India; Mireille Lobligeois has shown that the French government sponsored travels to India to this purpose. One of these travelers was Gonfreville, a dyer who had received his training at the Gobelin factory, and who was sent to Pondicherry (ruled by the French East India Company) in India (1827–30) to find out the techniques and methods used by Indian dyers and implement them in his factory in Rouen.[23] This is but one of many such travels to faraway places with the objective of collecting data.

Other French manufacturers looked for new techniques in regions closer by, the Levant or the Ottoman Empire, with which there were close commercial relations. In the various textile centers of the Ottoman Empire, as well, where Indian-style cloth was fashionable, new methods were being put into place to produce cloth that resembled that made in India.

"Egyptians Are Clumsy in Everything They Do"

Observers who visited the Ottoman Empire during the seventeenth and eighteenth centuries had a mixed attitude toward arts and crafts. Many of them had a critical discourse about what they saw. They were critical about the poor level of craftsmanship. There were repeated negative comments about the decline of the arts and crafts, writers often stressing the inabilities of local workmen and artisans and the poor quality of their work. Monsieur de Maillet, who was the French consul in Cairo for many years, wrote during the opening years of the eighteenth century that "les égyptiens aujourd'hui sont maladroit en tout," meaning that Egyptians were clumsy in everything they did, comments that were often repeated by others.[24] Referring to artisans who dyed cloth, Edmé François Jomard, who accompanied Napoleon in the Expedition, admitted that among the ancients, dyeing had been a very advanced craft, but at present, even though dyers produced good quality coloring, they only did so because they were following a blind routine.[25] Similarly for Vivant Denon, who claimed that artisans never invented anything new that might help them to improve their work, nor did they try to incorporate into their work the inventions of others.[26]

At the same time, another discourse focused on the methods and techniques, often unknown to them, which were used by local artisans and which aroused their curiosity. Many observers commented that the methods these craftsmen were using might well prove to be an improvement if used in French production. As these comments show, much of the French discourse in the eighteenth century was different from that being expressed a century later.

French sources give us a good idea of what interested the manufacturers and entrepreneurs. They were looking for ways of doing things that they thought were better done, or more cheaply and efficiently produced, in the various centers of the Ottoman Empire than in their own country. Sonnini, who visited Egypt in the last years of the eighteenth century, was very impressed with the use made of natron to bleach cloth, and he wrote that such efficient methods of bleaching should be tried out in France.[27] In a more general tone, Jean-Gabriel Peltier (1765–1825), a journalist at the time of the French Revolution, commenting on the findings of the savants of the Expedition, stated that the French often found practices unknown to them that could be usefully implemented in their own factories.[28]

Superiority of Ottoman Dyes

French producers were attempting to improve the process of coloring textiles, particularly dyeing and bleaching. Why? In the first place, colored textiles had become very fashionable, both in Europe and in the Ottoman Empire. Enormous quantities were imported from India to satisfy the market. In the eighteenth century, there were attempts to imitate them, both in the Ottoman Empire and in Europe, to answer the growing demand for this fashionable product, and presumably to produce them more cheaply.[29] In many parts of Europe during the seventeenth century, the desire to have a greater variety of colors for clothing seems to have expanded to middling classes. Whereas rich and varied colors in the past were mainly the domain of ruling classes and clergy, more and more, colored garments were becoming desirable to other segments of society.

In the second place, this trend was occurring at a time when the art of coloring cloth was to a large extent undeveloped. The methods and techniques of dyeing and bleaching in Egypt and other parts of the Ottoman Empire were, at the time, of far superior variety and quality to those in France or most parts of Europe. A study of dyes in early eighteenth-century England shows that colors were limited, and they were of poor quality. For textiles of good quality needing to be dyed, the cloth was sent to Holland to be bleached, a difficult and costly venture. A number of colors continued to be inaccessible for most people. Red dye, for instance, remained extremely expensive till the end of the eighteenth century.[30] In some cases, cotton cloth was sent to the Levant to be dyed red.[31] All this raise the price of colored cloth considerably, which explains why there was great interest in colors and dyes from the east.

French interest in Ottoman dyes raises an important issue of a more general nature about economic relationships. In the nineteenth century, colonial powers were particularly interested in obtaining cheap raw materials from the countries they colonized. In the present case, it was not raw materials that the French were looking for, but techniques of how to obtain the right colors, how to ensure that they were produced rapidly and at a reasonable cost, and how to make sure that they were fast colors that did not fade away when washed. Learning the know-how of Ottoman artisans was consequently just as important as importing the raw material.

The often-repeated statements on the decline of oriental craftsmanship are thus called into question. In the eighteenth century, there is, on the contrary, a recognition of the skills practiced by artisans in Ottoman lands and repeated attempts to imitate them. This dimension is often missing in the modernization paradigm as well as in the model of world systems, both of which portray Europe, or the core, as the space where there were skilled workers, and the rest of the world, or the periphery, as spaces of unskilled workers. It focuses on Europe's need for raw materials but tends to neglect its needs for these skills. This view of artisan skills challenges some of the basic precepts of these models and highlights the need to formulate new paradigms.

Learning the Skills of Dyeing

There are at least three domains in which the French were trying to obtain know-how from artisans in Egypt and other parts of the Ottoman Empire, all of them linked to the coloring of cloth.

The first of these domains was in the great variety of colors. According to Husam Abdul-Mu'ti's work, based on court records, dyers of cloth in Cairo were able to make a great variety of colors. According to Jomard, there were very few colors that these artisans could not produce. They were also versatile in the coloring of different types of cloth like silk or cotton, for which the coloring techniques had to be adapted. Girard, for example, noted that in the city of Mahalla al-Kubra, silk was dyed in red, black, green, sky blue, and dark blue, adding that only in Cairo were dyers able to produce a rose color.[32] In addition, the various localities where textiles were produced had their own specializations not only of cloth but also of color, with indigo being the most dominant.

Among the various colors, the one that seems to have interested the French producer most was red. It remained expensive to produce in Europe (in spite of the discovery of cochineal, which was brought from America); however, it was produced very commonly in the Ottoman Empire, in textile centers in Edirne, Izmir, Damascus, and Cairo. In Cairo there were two guilds whose specialization was to dye in the red color. One was the guild of dyers in red *(ta'ifat al-sabbaghin fi-l-ahmar)*; the second specialized in a particular red hue called *qandaqi (ta'ifat al-sabbaghin fi-l-qandaqi)*.

Sometimes guilds were even more specialized, as was noted by Abdul-Karim Rafeq, who writes of a guild in Aleppo (1627) that specialized in dyeing the linen of Malatya in red *(ta'ifat al-sabbaghin li-l-sabgh al-ahmar al-malti bi-Halab)*.[33]

Edirne and Izmir were major centers for the production of a particular kind of red dye, and textiles were sent there from Europe to be dyed in a red called *rouge d'Andrinople* or *rouge turc*, sometimes called in English "Turkey red." Andrinople, which gave its name to this color, was the European name for the town of Edirne. In Egypt, safflower was extensively used for this purpose. These examples suggest not only that the production of red was well-mastered in various Ottoman centers, but that, significantly, the techniques for its production probably differed between one center and another, and possibly even between one guild and another, reflecting a high level of diversity. It also reflects the local nature of many of these technologies, developed by artisans in accordance with the materials available to them in a particular locality.

A second domain was in the skill of dyeing one cloth in multiple colors. Together with the guilds that specialized in the dye of a single color, there was also a guild that specialized in multiple colors, and referred to as the "guild dyeing in colors like yellow, green, blue, *lazaward*, brown, and other colors."[34] The Swedish traveler Frederic Hasselquist, who visited Damietta between 1749 and 1752, noted this skill in the multicolored table napkins and other cloth, with stripes of white, blue, red, and yellow, which were exported to Turkey every year.[35]

A third domain was the art of bleaching. Until the end of the eighteenth century, in Europe, bleaching was an extremely long and costly process that took many weeks—a very expensive undertaking. There was more than one method used in the Ottoman Empire to bleach cloth. In Egypt, bleaching was done with natron and sal ammoniac *(nashadir)*; in the Levant, it was done with the technique of steaming. Compared with most European techniques (with the exception of those used by the Dutch), these were simple, efficient, and economic.

No wonder then that there were attempts to transfer these bleaching methods to France. Jean-Antoine-Claude Chaptal, a famous French chemist, studied the Egyptian procedure to produce sal ammoniac, which was used to help textiles keep their colors, experimenting further in order to produce it more economically.[36] Chaptal also published a work on the method used in the Levant for bleaching by vapor. This method of *blanchiment à la vapeur* was introduced in France from the Levant in the mid-eighteenth century, but it had been kept secret for some time.[37] Chaptal nevertheless claimed the credit for having himself introduced it in France, because it could be done rapidly and economically.[38]

Difficulties (and Solutions) in the Process of Transfer

Throughout the eighteenth century, there were efforts to appropriate the methods and techniques by French producers who wished to implement them in France. The process of transfer varied greatly. Some examples suggest that it may have been smooth at times. During the Napoleonic Expedition, for example, the conditions of a military occupation may have facilitated these transfers. That, in any case, is the impression one gets from the transfer of the technology of using safflower as a dye and of its fairly smooth and rapid use in France. Possibly too, the production of red by the use of safflower was a comparatively simpler process than other methods. It had one big advantage, namely that it was fast on the cloth without the need to use mordants.[39]

Safflower was known as a dye in Europe, and France imported significant quantities from Egypt throughout the eighteenth century. However, it was only used to dye silk. Attempts to use it to dye cotton and linen were unsuccessful. With the enormous expansion of the cotton trade and cotton production, this became a problem. At the time of the French Expedition, one of the chemists who accompanied Napoleon, Claude-Louis Berthollet (1748–1822), himself a chemist who had a great knowledge of dyes, visited a local dye workshop and watched the dyers closely for a few days to see how they dyed cloth with the safflower plant. He then wrote a detailed description of the process. In the years following the French Expedition, the Egyptian procedure for using safflower as a textile dye for cotton and linen was described in several manuals for dyers, written by dyers for the use of dyers, and in treatises on its manufacture so that dyers could implement the instructions; it also seems to have penetrated the practice in French manufactures.

But the process was not always so easy, and the transfer of know-how from Ottoman lands to Europe was often difficult. There were problems of various kinds, both technical and human, which slowed down the process.

One reason for this difficulty was the fact that what French manufacturers were interested in learning was in the domain of crafts practiced by artisans. However, these practices were not put down on paper. Whoever wanted to learn them had to be on the spot, observe carefully the way that things were done, and try to imitate what he saw. The results were mixed. At times, the transfers were slow, since it took time to learn and to appropriate these processes. Some met with failure, others with success.

Reticence of artisans to share their know-how

One of the difficulties was that, for the most part, artisans were not eager to share their know-how, specifically with strangers from outside the profession or guild. This was a way of protecting their craft and ensuring their livelihood, because they were afraid of competition, to a certain extent delaying the process of transfer. Therefore, at times, subterfuge methods were used to obtain information.

At the formal level, a few guilds explicitly forbade their members to divulge the secrets of their craft. In a case involving the guild of dyers in multiple colors dated 1082/1671, guild rules specifically mentioned that no member was to teach anyone their craft; they had learned to imitate the Indian style of decoration and wanted to have a monopoly of this craft.[40] Such explicit conditions were not necessarily the norm. Nevertheless, the general spirit of the guild was to keep the craft within the group, which created barriers to the smooth movement of know-how. Several curious travelers remarked on how difficult it was to penetrate the mysteries of artisans' work. Both Jean de Thevenot (1633–67), in the seventeenth century,[41] and Volney (1757–1820), in the eighteenth century,[42] stated that the Syrian artisans who produced leather goods of very high quality were extremely reticent when it came to talking about the methods of their work, keeping their techniques secret.

Similarly, in eighteenth-century Egypt, it could sometimes be difficult to find information about artisans' work. The example of sal ammoniac is illuminating. This product was in great demand in France because of its multiple uses in medical cures as well as in crafts and industries, and large amounts were purchased yearly from Egypt.

In an attempt to collect information on sal ammoniac in Egypt, a certain physician called M. Granger concealed his identity by dressing himself in Arab clothes and walking barefoot so as not to attract attention to himself as he observed and collected information about this product. He was undertaking what in our times would be called industrial espionage. He particularly gained confidence when he saved the life of a person who had taken an opium overdose, and he treated many patients. Only then was he able to obtain the information that he wanted on the secrets of this production.[43]

Hence, in many ways, the artisans of the Ottoman lands were not essentially different from artisans in Europe. In Europe, as in Egypt and Syria, competition between the producers pushed them to keep their working methods to themselves. When, for example, the technique to produce red dye was transferred from Edirne and Izmir to France, those who mastered it kept it a secret for many years. "Ceux qui ont réussi ne communiquent pas leur secret," wrote Le Pileur d'Appligny in 1776.[44] This complaint was often repeated.[45] The same secrecy was applied to the method for bleaching cotton, introduced about the mid-eighteenth century; those who learned it did not share it with others. The technique remained restricted to a few producers until Chaptal in the early nineteenth century published the process in an academic journal with a view to diffusing the secrets of this technology.[46]

The complexity of their techniques

Another difficulty for the transfer of know-how resided in the actual processes and the degree of complexity. Some of the techniques used by textile workers were quite complex, a fact which has not been given the recognition it deserves, to a large extent because one tends to associate crafts with simplicity, and complexity in production with machinery. However, even before industrialized production, some crafts, done by hand or through relatively simple tools, required a lot of skill and a high level of know-how. For Europeans who tried to find out the secrets of production it is apparent that at times there were enormous difficulties in understanding these techniques and in implementing the required know-how.

In this context, it is interesting to follow the stages, the difficulties, and the length of time it took the French to find out how sal ammoniac was produced in Egypt and how to reproduce it in their own country. Sal ammoniac is a product found in nature, usually in the vicinity of volcanoes, but in relatively small quantities. By contrast, its production had been mastered by artisans, and consequently Egypt was the only country where it was a man-made product. As a result, Egypt had a quasi-monopoly of this commodity in international markets.[47] It disposed of large amounts that were exported to many destinations because of the multiple uses to which it could be put. There were a number of workshops, mostly in the Delta area, some of them relatively large. The one in the town of Mansura employed thirty workers.[48] Several others were in the towns of Damir, Damanhur, Baranbal, and others. There were also two workshops in Cairo and Bulaq. Girard counted a total of sixteen workshops for the production of sal ammoniac in Egypt.[49]

By the beginning of the eighteenth century, French travelers to Egypt, realizing that sal ammoniac was actually being produced in this country, tried to find out where it could be found and how it was made. They made repeated attempts to find out the secrets of its production. About 1716, a certain Geoffroy, who had spent some time in Egypt, read a paper on sal ammoniac to the Académie des Sciences, which he published in 1720. The Académie became interested in this matter and, wanting to find out more about its production, asked the French consul in Cairo for detailed reports. The consul, in his turn, turned to a Jesuit priest resident in Egypt, Père Sicard. This Jesuit had resided in the region for many years; he knew the Arabic language and seems to have had numerous local contacts. Père Sicard's main duty in Egypt was to spread the Gospel. He nevertheless agreed to undertake this information-gathering mission, writing his final report with the details of production in 1722, shortly after which he died in Cairo.[50]

Neither Père Sicard nor any of his predecessors in this venture were quite aware of the complexities of the operations required to obtain this product. Clearly the information that he gathered was lacking or unclear, since shortly thereafter, another envoy was sent from France for this same purpose of collecting information on the production of sal ammoniac.

This time it was M. Granger, a physician sent by the French monarch in 1730. It took him a long while to fulfill his mission, and he eventually sent his report on the production on sal ammoniac in 1735 to the Académie des Sciences in Paris.

At the end of the century, Berthollet, a member of the Napoleonic Expedition, with the eyes of an expert chemist, read all these reports very carefully, and he found them to be so contradictory and incomplete that it was impossible to implement their findings. He had himself a few years earlier in his laboratory work in France identified an acid, chlorine, that could be used as a bleach (which it still is to this day).[51] Subsequently, while in Egypt, he found out that it was a main element in sal ammoniac. During his stay in Egypt, he analyzed this sal ammoniac closely and found out more details of its composition that earlier French observers had not noted. His eye could see what his predecessors had not noticed because, by coincidence, he was familiar from his laboratory research with the acid the sal ammoniac contained.

One reason for the inaccuracies of the information in these reports was that the data were collected by people with little or no knowledge of the crafts or the techniques they wrote about. Nevertheless, by the early years of the nineteenth century, Jean-Antoine Chaptal could write, "Now we know all about it and can produce it here economically."[52] But this process had taken a little less than a century to be implemented.

Another example that stands out is that of the red dye called "Andrinople red," used for fashionable printed cottons; it was produced in Edirne, Thessaly, and Izmir, and was very much in demand in Europe because of the brightness of the color. It appears that the process was long and complex.[53] This Andrinople red or "Turkey red" was made out of the madder plant. Although the madder plant was known in Europe as a red dye, the process of making the Andrinople red, known to be of much better quality, was distinguished from ordinary madder red by the length and complexity of the process needed to obtain it.[54] The repeated attempts to imitate this particular red dye clearly show that the transfer of know-how implied not only the importation of raw materials; rather it was the skills needed to make best use of this material. The transfer of this know-how was consequently a slow and costly business, and Europeans made multiple attempts to obtain the know-how of its processes by numerous channels, even sending spies and transferring artisans.

Ottoman artisans in Europe

The eighteenth century witnessed repeated transfers of textile artisans from the Ottoman Empire to Europe, France, the Hapsburg Empire, and Amsterdam, with the purpose of introducing their working techniques to European factories.[55] These transfers of artisans in different parts of the world were an important tool for the circulation and transfer of techniques in various domains at a time when there was competition between countries to find new ways to improve production. They were at times undertaken at the initiatives of governments, factory owners, or entrepreneurs, at other times at the initiative of the craftsmen themselves, individual artisans who on their own accord moved to another town where they could practice their craft. Liliane Hilaire-Perez considered such exchanges to be one of the factors that helped shape the Industrial Revolution.[56]

This movement of artisans from the Ottoman Empire to Europe was part of a familiar pattern in the early modern period. The objective of these moves, especially in the eighteenth century, was to circulate know-how and technology in a world in which competition was growing between rival groups; in which a process of industrialization had started; and in which, more and more, local forms of knowledge were being globalized. These moves were commonly practiced in Europe—artisans traveling from England to France, for instance, to teach workers the skills that they knew.[57] Liliane Hilaire-Perez studied artisans who were transferred from England to France in 1718 to teach watchmaking and metalwork to French factory workers in Paris and Normandy.[58] She showed that this was fairly common in eighteenth-century Europe, as economies were developing and industries starting to emerge.

Nor were these transfers from Ottoman lands to Europe essentially different from the transfers of artisans that took place in the early nineteenth century under Muhammad Ali. His initiative to bring in European workers was portrayed as a novelty. When this ruler opened new factories, he hired a number of foreign workers to teach local artisans their know-how, some of them from Languedoc, France, for the manufacture of drapes; from Istanbul for the silk industry; from Tunis to teach local artisans to make the fez;[59] and indigo dyers from India to teach local dyers their craft.[60] He was in fact following a pattern that had been in vogue for at least a century.

French sources contain significant information with regard to the transfer of artisans from the Ottoman Empire to Europe in the eighteenth century, from Edirne, Izmir, and Istanbul to different towns and cities in France, Amsterdam, and the Hapsburg Empire, mainly in order to teach local workers the art of dyeing textiles. Entrepreneurs and factory owners helped in these transfers in order to bring artisans with skills to work in their factories.

Among the earliest was a group of Armenians who settled in Marseilles, among whom was a group of dyers around the 1660s. Shortly after, a number of Greek artisans who worked with this dye arrived in Languedoc. At first they kept their method secret, but soon after, the techniques they used became known to others.[61] In 1747, a number of manufacturers brought in Greek dyers working in Edirne or Andrinople to work in their factories in Rouen and in Darnetal for the same purpose, and soon afterward the factory was producing printed textiles using this *rouge d'Andrinople*.[62] In Normandy, this same pattern was repeated as Greek artisans introduced the methods for this special red dye.[63]

In spite of these numerous artisan transfers, the process for producing Andrinople red remained difficult to imitate. Those who mastered the technique kept it to themselves while the others who did not have direct access to these techniques often failed in their experiments. A certain M. Kuhlman, in spite of his repeated experiments to get red dye, could, as late as 1823, only get a violet color, indicating that the process of transfer of know-how was extremely slow and faced considerable difficulties, if we consider that the first group of artisans who were transferred to France for this purpose arrived sometime in the mid-seventeenth century.[64]

Many of these French manufacturers for printed cottons, however, were not successful and many had to close soon after they were established. Toward the end of the eighteenth century, Pierre Jaubert estimated that of about a hundred factories that were opened, some eighty were shut down, either because they were unable to produce designs, or they could not imitate the *indiennes* in a satisfactory way.[65] This situation could explain why, even though the French had introduced printed cottons quite a while earlier, sometime in the mid-seventeenth century, we learn from Girard at the end of the eighteenth century that at the time of the Napoleonic Expedition, the French were still importing cottons decorated with Indian designs made in Cairo. Wages in Cairo may have been a factor, as well as the fact that cotton was, by the eighteenth century, being locally grown in considerable quantities.[66]

State Support and Publications

In part, the success of many of these enterprises was due to the facilities that the French state provided and its encouragement of local industries. It was visible at different stages of the process of transfer. Voyages to textiles centers, to the Ottoman Empire, India, and Persia, were sometimes state-sponsored with the aim of collecting information that might help advance production. There was some sort of state support when artisans were brought in to work in French factories. Factory owners demanded that the state make provisions in order to give these artisans legal status and permanent residence for them and their families, especially in the face of local guild members who could potentially create problems for them. In some cases it did so. In December 1756, for instance, a royal edict was issued in favor of two brothers, François and Jean-Claude Flachat, owners of a factory specializing in dyeing cloth in Saint Chaumond. The edict, which gave them exclusive rights to dye cotton cloth in Andrinople red, made their factory a *manufacture royal*. The workers they got from abroad would become naturalized after three years' work and had a lifelong tax exemption. The objective of the state in providing these facilities was to limit importations.[67] Thus the producers of these textiles could count on the support of the state in its initiatives to improve production in the face of competitors.

However, these very same manufacturers, who had often appropriated the techniques practiced among Ottoman artisans with the support of the state or of the monarch, were nevertheless eager to keep the secrets of their technology to themselves. To maintain their advantage in the face of their competitors, they tried by every means to keep their production secrets to themselves and, for a while, this secrecy helped them to maintain a competitive edge against their rivals.

They soon, however, had to confront state policies that worked to their disadvantage. The French state wished to diffuse any technical knowledge that might help French industries and encourage their development. Thus, the state policies, which had for a long time been beneficial to these manufacturers, now became a threat. In the opening years of the nineteenth century, the French state started to publish specialized pamphlets and periodicals with the aim of helping French industry in its competition with the British. It was hoped that these publications would encourage and diffuse innovations in industry. The Société d'encouragement de l'industrie nationale, for instance, was founded in 1801 with the purpose of helping France in its Industrial Revolution against its main competitor, Britain. Among the prominent members of this Société were a number of the savants who had come to Egypt with Napoleon: Monge, Berthollet, Conte, and Jomard. Chaptal was also one of its active members and ardent supporters.[68]

The Société launched a periodical in 1802. The publication of the numerous manuals and guides for dyers as of the early nineteenth century helped to break the secrecy that producers had been able to impose for relatively long periods. These manuals for dyers contained detailed technical information on the craft. For instance, the 1819 edition of the *Nouveau Manuel du Teinturier* had a subtitle, "Guide Pratique des Apprentis et des ouvriers dans l'art de la teinture," and was written by one Baillot, a master dyer *(maître teinturier)*.[69]

With the multiplication of such publications, it became more difficult for a manufacturer to keep his techniques secret. The details of how to produce the red color called *rouge d'Andrinople*, which had created numerous problems for dyers, had become public knowledge. The guidebook for dyers provided the minute details of its production. In addition to this practical information, a more academic literature emerged written by chemists who linked the art of dyeing to chemistry. Among the most important were Berthollet and Chaptal, but there were many others, such as J.B. Vitalis, a professor of science and member of the Academy of Science, who wrote a guidebook on dyeing from a scientific rather than an artisanal perspective. His goal was to improve the art of dyeing.[70] The literature in question, whether artisanal or academic, helped the new techniques, whether those coming from Egyptian or Ottoman artisans, or from other sources, to become integrated into French industry.

Did These Transfers Ultimately Have Any Weight?

Penetration into important industries

It is difficult to measure the impact that these transfers of artisan know-how from the Ottoman Empire had. One has to find indirect ways in order to observe how they could have had some kind of short-term or long-term effect on the receivers of this know-how. One answer could lie in the fact that a number of important and well-known industries adapted and appropriated some of the techniques that had an Egyptian or Levantine origin. For instance, the Oberkampf manufacture, established in Jouy near Paris in 1760, was a top producer of printed textiles; it was given the title of *manufacture royale* in 1783 by Louis XVI. Enormous in size for its time, it employed close to a thousand workers at the end of the eighteenth century. Berthollet, Chaptal, Monge, and others who were familiar with various textile bleaching and dyeing techniques used in the Ottoman Empire apparently paid frequent visits to Jouy, bringing with them samples of cloth from Egypt, Syria, or Anatolia, so that they could be imitated in this factory.[71] The Oberkampf manufacture came to make use of some of the methods of Levantine or Ottoman origin, both in bleaching, where the *blanchiment à la vapeur* was used and improved upon, and in its *rouge d'Andrinople*.

The art of dyeing a piece of cloth in multiple colors also penetrated luxury French industry. After years of experimenting on how to achieve this art and incorporate artisan techniques in a manufacture, a machine was invented which could dye many colors in a single piece of cloth. This invention was linked to the royal manufacture of great renown, the Gobelin Royal Manufacture, to which was attached the *École Royale de Teinture de Gobelin*. In 1819, its director, Conte de Marillac, made a spectacular demonstration in front of all his former students of the use of new machines for dyeing pieces of cloth in different colors.[72]

Likewise, with the use of the henna plant as a dye, we can trace a similar pattern. This plant has long been known in Egypt for its coloring properties, where it was commonly used to dye hair and hands, in addition to cloth. The French only found out that it could be a textile dye after the Napoleonic Expedition to Egypt, under the initiative of Berthollet and Descotils, who described the procedure for obtaining a dye; their work spread very rapidly in France.[73] There then followed numerous experiments on henna, and it came to be used to dye silk into a brilliant black color in the silk industry of Lyon, the most important silk-producing city in France. It was referred to as *henne des arabes*. The owners of a silk factory in Lyon, Messrs. Gillet and Tabourin, obtained a *brevet d'invention* in September 1858, which allowed them to monopolize this technique for fifteen years.[74] In the years that followed, Mr. Gillet imported some eighty thousand kilos of henna annually for his factory, mainly from Algeria and Morocco.[75]

Beginning of the Nineteenth Century: The Loss of Several Monopolies

The procedure for multiple colors, the production of certain red colors, and procedures for cheaper and quicker methods of bleaching eventually penetrated French industry.

The integration of these technologies into the French textile industry was a factor that may have helped maintain its status as producer of luxury goods, especially in light of the competition over markets with Britain.

In the eighteenth century, as the Industrial Revolution was underway, it was clearly Britain that led the way, and it became hard for any producer to compete with the cheaper prices of its mass-produced textiles. French industry, in part due to the many political upheavals of the nineteenth century, tended to lag somewhat behind, a delay that increased during the disruptive years of the French Revolution and the period that followed. In order to increase its competitiveness, French industry moved toward the production of luxury items, of which those of the Oberkampf factory and the silk textiles of Lyon were examples. Both of these had made use of coloring techniques learned from artisans in Ottoman lands. For a long time France was able, in spite of numerous setbacks, to maintain its position as a major exporter of luxury items.[76]

Ultimately, however, these transfers of know-how brought about a lesser dependence on Levantine and Egyptian markets. As the nineteenth century progressed, the French were planting safflower; they were producing sal ammoniac. The red of Andrinople, which had been a monopoly of the towns of Izmir and Edirne, was being produced in France, and from there it was transferred to Scotland where a Frenchman, Monsieur Papillon, established a dyehouse that specialized in dyeing Andrinople red.[77] Thus, these transfers brought about an economic loss to Ottoman industries and had a negative effect on artisans. And eventually, the precious sal ammoniac in which Egypt had excelled, and which had for long been a major export item, was also starting to be produced in Europe.

For those techniques that did succeed, their origin was often forgotten. When Jack Goody wrote his book *The Theft of History*, he did not dwell much upon the Middle East, the Arab world, or the Ottoman world. And yet much of what he wrote has an echo in the themes elaborated above. Goody wrote about the appropriation by the west of certain values like humanism and rationality, which many writers had claimed were purely European in origin. He found these values in many other societies beyond Europe. He found that institutions such as democracy, mercantilism, capitalism, and individualism, linked to the modernization of the west, in fact had a much wider geographical spread in human societies. However, these values were appropriated by Europeans and presented as theirs.[78]

A similar line of thought can be applied, not only to abstract concepts, but to much more concrete conditions. It is possible to trace the process by which the identity of those who initiated the techniques that were transferred in the course of the eighteenth century was lost; the place from which they originated tended to fall with the passage of time into oblivion. Part of the reason was that the names of local artisans who had practiced the techniques had never been known or recorded. Part of the reason was that credit was given to the persons who had made the techniques known, or had written about them, or had been involved in the transfer process. Thus, the method for the preparation of safflower in order to use it for red dye was described by the Swedish traveler Hasselquist in the mid-eighteenth century; at the end of the century,

Berthollet again provided a detailed description. Soon after, however, this procedure was referred to as "*la façon Hasselquist*," with no mention of where Hasselquist had found it or to the fact that he had described what he had seen rather than invented it himself.[79] About a century after Ottoman artisans were transferred from Edirne and Izmir to the town of Darnetal to teach workers how to produce Andrinople red, Jean-Marie Roland de la Platière refers to the "discovery" in Darnetal of the red dye. In the process of transfer it had become known as *rouge de Darnetal*. The author does add, however, that it never reached the quality of Andrinople red.[80] The names of the local artisans in Cairo, Izmir, and Istanbul had never been mentioned. It was those who had transmitted these techniques whose names were recorded and remembered.

An excellent example of this trend is Berthollet, the chemist of the Napoleonic Expedition, who had spent much time observing and recording the practices that he found, many of which were subsequently diffused to France. A nineteenth-century biography of great men includes a few (unnumbered) pages about him and highly praises his great achievements, which benefited not only France but all of Europe: his studies of safflower, henna, and pastel colors; his study of the natron lakes from which man-made muriatic acid was extracted in a procedure that was unknown in Europe; and his realization of the importance of this product for European cloth bleaching.[81] Praises were bestowed on him for these discoveries, and he was given the merit almost as if he had been the inventor of these techniques.

With regard to bleaching by vapor, likewise, a similar process is evident. A book published in 1801 informs us that this technique reached France from the Levant at the same time as the red dye of *rouge d'Andrinople*, and had taken root in the south of France in the mid-eighteenth century; Chaptal claimed he was the one who introduced this Levantine technique to France, presumably in the early nineteenth century.[82] By the second half of the nineteenth century, its origins had become vague and confused. In the mid-nineteenth century, Louis Figuier, referring to two factories built before 1789, writes that the identity of the person who invented bleaching by vapor was not known, but that this technique originated in India at an unknown time. That the French borrowed this technique from the Levant is not mentioned. The name linked to it was that of Chaptal.[83] When, shortly after, the information about this new technique to bleach cotton reached England, the Englishmen started making trials of the "Chaptal procedure" in order to improve their manufactures.[84] In short, from the Levant, bleaching by vapor was spreading to different parts of Europe but with a different appellation.

Conclusion

Changing the direction

During the latter part of the nineteenth century, artificial dyes were invented, and soon they were being applied to textile industries. Consequently, the earlier dyes that European entrepreneurs and factory owners had tried so hard to imitate from the practices of artisans in the Ottoman Empire lost much of their relevance. Until then, these practices had become part and parcel of the processes that were eventually used in factories. This means that for close to two centuries, roughly from the mid-seventeenth to the end of the eighteenth century, the transfers of technology were taking place from south to north, rather than the other way around. That was a time when transfers in the opposite direction were fairly minimal. Only during the opening years of the nineteenth century, with the rule of Muhammad Ali, did west-to-east transfers pick up.

Artisan-scholar debate

Moreover, these east-to-west or south-to-north transfers form an excellent example of the way that the know-how of artisans in Cairo, Istanbul, or Izmir penetrated Europe in the early modern and modern period and that semiliterate artisans with certain skills potentially had an impact on French industry. Some of the traditional methods practiced by local artisans with regard to textile production were adapted and incorporated into modern scientific practice. Much in the same way, the cures that local eye doctors had elaborated for the treatment of ophthalmia were integrated into medical practice in nineteenth-century Europe and the techniques to produce sal ammoniac developed in Egypt by illiterate or semiliterate craftsmen were developed and taken over by European factories, first in Scotland (1856) before spreading to other places. The interaction between artisan and scholar, between empirical and theoretical or practical and academic, and between the local and the universal, took different forms and implicated various academies of sciences in Europe as well as scientists and master craftsmen who worked on the development of these imported techniques.

In the course of a complex process of transfer, people like Berthollet played the role of intermediary between craftsman and scientist. He had had the necessary scientific training before coming to Egypt, and therefore had a more analytic way of assessing what he saw, by comparison with earlier observers like Sicard, Granger, or Hasselquist. During his stay, Berthollet was both a close observer of the artisan techniques he witnessed in Cairo, and a reliable interpreter of what he saw on the basis of the theoretical training he had had, hence his ability to link the practical with the theoretical.

These findings about artisan practices as a source in the formation of modern science and technology are in keeping with recent scholarship about the emergence of modern sciences in sixteenth- to seventeenth-century Europe. These works study the relationship of craft traditions and science. They ask whether the Scientific Revolution was the result only of great intellectuals and learned academics searching for the universal laws of nature, whether there was a place for empirical knowledge, or whether scientific knowledge required a combination of theoretical works together with the practice of artisans. Recent scholarship tends to emphasize the contribution of artisans as an essential element in the creation of modern science because they brought in their empirical experience, which was based on their daily practice and experiment.[85] They challenge the claim that modern science and technology were the fruit only of the efforts of great men, of scientists who had an intellectual or academic background, who experimented in laboratories, and whose learning found its way into books. James A. Secord considers that specific practices taking place in specific locations were at the source of scientific development. In order to understand how science developed, one had to study practice.[86]

Thus, one finds parallels in the artisan-versus-scholar relationship between these examples cited here and other similar ones taking place in other countries. Here, one is reminded of the statements of E.P.

Thompson when he writes that the Industrial Revolution would hardly have developed had it not been for the diverse skills of English workers, anonymous and forgotten.[87] His work has inspired many others. Vincent Ilardi's recent study, for instance, shows that the influence of unlettered but skilled artisans working on glass lenses in Florence and Venice during the Renaissance was the basis of advances in lens technology that eventually led to the telescope.[88] One can therefore place the transfers of Ottoman artisans' know-how in a similar context.

These studies indicate that we need to rethink some of the ways in which these "traditional craftsmen" have been viewed. The role that they potentially played in modern developments should also be reassessed, taking into consideration that section of the picture that history books have forgotten to mention and shedding light on the efforts of the anonymous artisan, who initiated his techniques and know-how through trial and error and through his daily practice.

Early modern exchange

On a broader level, these transfers of know-how practiced by artisans in Cairo, Aleppo, Izmir, or Istanbul, who worked in textile production, were part of a worldwide, large-scale transfer of technology from east to west during the sixteenth to the eighteenth centuries. They had parallels with the transfers of technical skills, especially in textile production, from India to England. David Washbrook, who studied these transfers, noted that Indian weavers provided English industry with the techniques of designing and weaving cotton.[89] Such transfers, in the words of Washbrook, challenge the claims that modern history was made by Europe alone.[90]

Local to global

In the process, what had, possibly for centuries, been local knowledge, developed and practiced in particular localities in answer to their specific needs, was in the process of becoming standardized in the eighteenth and nineteenth centuries, or in other words, becoming part of more globalized forms of knowledge. As this process developed, elements that were of a local nature lost their particularity. And the global became somewhat associated with the west. The transfers of knowledge from artisans of the Ottoman Empire can consequently be seen as part of the early stages of the globalization of knowledge.

The need of Europeans to obtain technical know-how from the east decreased as the century progressed. In the latter part of the nineteenth century, more and more transfers were taking place in the other direction, from Europe to the east. The end of the nineteenth century was also the period during which colonial rule, with its mission for progress and civilization, extended over larger regions and penetrated deeper into local economies.

The discourse on the transfers of knowledge underwent a change as conditions on the ground changed, and Europe's hegemonic position emerged and was consolidated. The statements on what the French could learn from Cairo artisans tended to be replaced by those on the civilizing mission that European civilization could bring to so-called 'backward' countries.

In the meantime, the history of the east–west transfers was to a large extent forgotten. The ideology of colonialism had gained the upper hand over the realities of historical development. By the end of the nineteenth century, the notion of transfer of knowledge came more and more to be seen as a one-way move, linked to this colonialist ideology.

5 Epilogue

Colonial histories have tended to distort the history of the so-called 'Third World' countries during the period prior to their colonization, developing a particular lens through which these histories were written. By removing this lens, one can propose a different way of seeing history. This book is an attempt to try out a paradigm that allows us to rethink the history of Egypt during the crucial period that preceded European penetration. It offers an alternative to the decline paradigm, which for a long time dominated historical studies of this period.

For Egypt, as for many parts of the world, the centuries between 1500 and 1800 were transformative. To a certain extent, the transformations in question were linked to worldwide trends that were initiated by the expansion in world trade and the creation of maritime routes that linked, in a regular manner, most parts of the world. The book elaborates on the consequences of these transformations. It identifies some of the domains in which both the European and the non-European worlds underwent similar trends and patterns. One example is a higher level of commercialization than in earlier periods. This was manifested in various ways. At the level of culture, for instance, a more commercial culture affected the way that language was used. Written texts made extensive use of a register that was close to the spoken word, and they thus became more accessible to those who were outside the educational establishment.

This trend toward the vernacular coincided with parallel trends in several other parts of the world, both in Europe and in Asia, where local dialects became acceptable forms of written communication.

Similar trends, at the level of the economy, were seen in the production and trade of textiles. The worldwide expansion in textiles, especially in cotton cloth, touched many regions of the world in one way or another. It also had an impact on the production of artisans in Egypt. Those among them who wove these cotton textiles expanded their production, especially in the eighteenth century, adjusting guild rules that might hamper their activities. As a result, they were able to attain a place in the world trade in cloth, because they were able to address particular markets. A considerable portion of the textiles that were exported was coarse, colorless cloth, priced relatively low, and aimed at a modest to poor population. Thus, different aspects of economy and culture were affected by the conditions of the period.

What does this mean for our understanding of Egyptian history? One way to answer this complex question is to posit a shift that brought some sectors of society, economy, and culture closer than other sectors to worldwide conditions. And if that was the case, this shift would also tend to distance them from their surroundings. The repercussions of this trend would be more clearly felt subsequently as the push toward globalization increased and touched more sectors. The period, especially the latter part, could be seen as one with growing hybridity, with multiple economic and cultural patterns, systems, or modes coexisting at the same time as new methods and approaches came into the picture and were, with varying degrees of success, integrated into existing patterns of thought or work.

One can also change one's angle by shifting the lens, in social terms, from above to below. Today, most world histories are written at the macro level. This book proposes a method to write world history as "history from below" and to make links between the big picture of major world transformations and the ordinary anonymous people whose names never appear in history books. It is a method that can surely be applied to other countries or regions. The contributions of numerous unnamed artisans and tradesmen have as yet to be given their rightful value. They too were, in their own ways, transformative. The techniques they used, their technologies that evolved on the basis of practice, or trial and error, all these also had some impact on modern world history, as they were transferred to Europe and integrated into manufacturing in France and elsewhere. As potential consumers of a vernacularized form of writing, they may have contributed to the expansion of texts written in an accessible language. Thus, the paradigm suggested in this book allows us not only to rethink the period from 1500 to 1800 but also to understand the nineteenth century in a different way.

The period from 1500 to 1800 was crucial in the formation of the world we live in today. Its making was part of a complex process involving multiple regions and multiple parties. This book proposes a way to consider the world's transformations during this period—not only the developments in Europe and by Europeans, but also those of the non-European world. Egypt and other non-European societies have their own histories that need to be explored and understood, certainly in order to understand their own dynamism but also, more broadly, to place them in the context of the transformations of the period from 1500 to 1800 to which they contributed.

Dating System of the French Revolution

Republican Year	Started on
I	22 September 1792
II	22 September 1793
III	22 September 1794
IV	23 September 1795
V	22 September 1796
VI	22 September 1797
VII	22 September 1798
VIII	23 September 1799
IX	23 September 1800
X	23 September 1801
XI	23 September 1802
XII	24 September 1803
XIII	23 September 1804
XIV	23 September 1805

Source: Wikipedia

Notes

Chapter 1

1 Frank W. Thackeray and John E. Findling, eds., *Events that Formed the Modern World*, vol. 1, *From the European Renaissance through the Sixteenth Century* (Santa Barbara: ABC-CLIO, 2012).

2 Quoted by Jack Goody, *The Theft of History* (Cambridge: Cambridge University Press, 2008), 1.

3 Toby E. Huff, *Intellectual Curiosity and the Scientific Revolution: A Global Perspective* (Cambridge: Cambridge University Press, 2011), 7–9.

4 Quoted in D.E. Mungello, *The Great Encounter of China and the West 1500–1800* (Lanham, MD: Rowman and Littlefield, 2013), 3.

5 Michael Adas, "Contested Hegemony: The Great War and the Afro-Asian Assault on the Civilizing Mission Ideology," *Journal of World History* 15, no. 1 (March 2004): 31–63; Mathew Burrows, "*Mission Civilisatrice*: French Cultural Policy in the Middle East, 1860–1914," *The Historical Journal* 29, no. 1 (1986): 109–35; Michael Mann, "'Torch Bearers upon the Path of Progress,' Britain's Ideology of a Moral and Material Progress in India: An Introductory Essay," in *Colonialism as a Civilizing Mission: Cultural Ideology in British India*, ed. Harald Fischer-Tine and Michael Mann (London: Anthem Press, 2004), 4–10.

6 Prasannan Parthasarathi, *The Transition to a Colonial Economy: Weavers, Merchants, and Kings in South India, 1720–1800* (Cambridge: Cambridge University Press, 2001), 3.

7 John F. Richards, "Early Modern India and World History," *Journal of World History* 8, no. 2 (Fall 1997): 197–209.

8 Peter Gran, *Beyond Eurocentrism: A New View of World History* (Syracuse, NY: Syracuse University Press, 1996), 2–7.

9 Samir Amin, *Global History: A View from the South* (Cape Town: Pambazuka Press, 2011), 6–7; "Colonialism and the Rise of Capitalism: A Comment," *Science & Society* 54, no. 1 (Spring 1990): 67–72.

10 J.M. Blaut, "Diffusionism: A Uniformitarian Critique," *Annals of the Association of American Geographers* 77, no. 1 (March 1987): 30–47.

11 Eric Wolf, *Europe and the People without History* (Berkeley: University of California Press, 2010); Goody, *The Theft of History*; André Gunder Frank, *ReOrient: Global Economy in the Asian Age* (Berkeley: University of California Press, 1998).

12 David Washbrook, "From Comparative Sociology to Global History: Britain and India in the Pre-History of Modernity," *Journal of the Economic and Social History of the Orient* 40, no. 4 (1997): 410–43.

13 Christopher A. Bayly, *The Birth of the Modern World, 1780–1914* (Oxford: Blackwell, 2004), 471.

14 Eric Williams, *Capitalism and Slavery* (Chapel Hill: University of North Carolina Press, 1944); Timothy Mitchell, "The State of Modernity," in *Questions of Modernity*, ed. Timothy Mitchell (Toronto: University of Toronto Press, 1994), 2–3; Giancarlo Casale, *The Ottoman Age of Exploration* (New York: Oxford University Press, 2010).

15 Suraiya Faroqhi, *The Ottoman Empire and the World around It* (London: I.B.Tauris, 2004); Daniel Goffman, *The Ottoman Empire and Early Modern Europe* (Cambridge: Cambridge University Press, 2002); Casale, *The Ottoman Age of Exploration.*

16 Bayly, *The Birth of the Modern World*, 42, 470–72; Romain Bertrand, *Histoire à parts égales: Récits d'une rencontre Orient–Occident (XVIe–XVIIe siècle)* (Paris: Editions du Seuil, 2011), 12.

17 His ideas were elaborated in *Artisans et commerçants au Caire au XVIIIe siècle*, 2 vols. (Damascus: Institut français de Damas, 1974).

18 Richard Rapp, "The Unmaking of the Mediterranean Trade Hegemony: International Trade Rivalry and the Commercial Revolution," *The Journal of Economic History* 35, no. 5 (1975): 499–525.

19 Immanuel Wallerstein elaborated his model in a three-volume work entitled *The Modern World System* (Berkeley: University of California Press, 2011).

20 Mehmet Bulut, "The Role of the Ottomans and the Dutch in the Commercial Integration between the Levant and the Atlantic in the Seventeenth Century," *Journal of the Ecoomic and Social History of the Orient* 45, no. 2 (2002): 197–230.
21 Charles Parker, *Global Interactions in the Early Modern Age, 1400–1800* (New York: Cambridge University Press, 2010), 2–11.
22 Roger Owen, *Cotton and the Egyptian Economy, 1820–1914: A Study in Trade and Development* (Oxford: Clarendon, 1969), 175.
23 Gilles Veinstein, "Commercial Relations between India and the Ottoman Empire (Late Fifteenth to Late Eighteenth Century): A Few Notes and Hypothesis," in *Merchants, Companies and Trade: Europe and Asia in the Early Modern Era*, ed. Suchil Chaudhury and Michel Morineau (Cambridge: Cambridge University Press, 1999), 95–115.
24 Scott Cameron Levi, *The Indian Diaspora in Central Asia and Its Trade, 1550–1900* (Leiden: Brill, 2001), 34–35; see also Veinstein, "Commercial Relations between India and the Ottoman Empire," 102–107.
25 Jean-Claude Flachat, *Observations sur le commerce et sur les arts*, vol. 2 (Lyon: Chez Jacquenod père et Rusand, 1766), 270–75.
26 Jacques Peuchet, *Bibliothèque commercial*, vol. 2 (Paris: Chez Buisson, Juillet 1803), 39.
27 Adolphe-Jérôme Blanqui, *Dictionnaire du Commerce et de l'industrie*, vol. 1 (Brussels: Imprimerie A. Cauvin, 1837), 68.
28 Frank, *ReOrient*, 201.
29 Suraiya Faroqhi, "Immigrant Tradesmen as Guild Members, or the Adventures of Tunisian Fez-sellers in Eighteenth-century Istanbul," in *The Arab Lands in the Ottoman Era (1600–1900): In Honor of Caesar Farah*, ed. Jane Hathaway (Minneapolis: Center of Early Modern History, 2009), 187–207.
30 Suraiya Faroqhi, "Declines and Revivals in Textile Production," in *Cambridge History of Turkey: The Later Ottoman Empire, 1603–1839*, vol. 3, ed. Suraiya Faroqhi (Cambridge: Cambridge University Press, 2006), 366.
31 R.J. Barendse, *The Arabian Sea: The Indian Ocean World of the Seventeenth Century* (New York: Sharpe, Inc., 2002), 6–7.
32 Raymond, *Artisans et commerçants.*
33 Joseph Fletcher, "Integrative History: Parallels and Interconnections in the Early Modern Period, 1500–1800," *Journal of Turkish Studies* 9 (1985): 37–57.

34 Bayly, *The Birth of the Modern World*, 41–42.
35 Nelly Hanna, *Artisan Entrepreneurs in Cairo and Early Modern Capitalism (1600–1800)* (Syracuse, NY: Syracuse University Press, 2011).
36 Hanna, *Artisan Entrepreneurs*, 162.
37 Sevket Pamuk, *A Monetary History of the Ottoman Empire* (Cambridge: Cambridge University Press, 2000), xix.
38 Jon Mandaville, "Usurious Piety: The Cash Waqf Controversy in the Ottoman Empire," *International Journal of Middle East Studies* 10, no. 3 (Aug. 1979): 289–308.
39 Frank Perlin, "Monetary Revolution and Societal Change in the Late Medieval and Early Modern Times: A Review Article," *The Journal of Asian Studies* 45, no. 5 (Nov. 1986): 1037–49; Washbrook, "Merchants, Markets and Commerce in Early Modern Southern India," *Journal of the Economic and Social History of the Orient* 53 (2010): 271.
40 Hanna, *Artisan Entrepreneurs in Cairo*, 166–67.
41 Kenneth M. Cuno, "Ideology and Juridical Discourse in Ottoman Egypt: The Use of the Concept of *Irsad*," *Islamic Law and Society* 6, no. 2 (1999): 136–63.
42 Cuno, "Ideology and Juridical Discourse," 139.
43 Baer, "The Waqf as a Prop for the Social System (Sixteenth to Twentieth Centuries)," *Islamic Law and Society* 4, no. 3 (1997): 284–85.
44 Sami Zubaida, *Law and Power in the Islamic World* (London: I.B.Tauris, 2003), 112.
45 Nelly Hanna, *Artisan Entrepreneurs*, 167–69; Hanna, "Guild Waqf: Between Religious Law and Common Law," in *Held in Trust*, ed. Pascale Ghazaleh (Cairo: American University in Cairo Press, 2011), 165–89.
46 Peter Gran, *Islamic Roots of Capitalism: Egypt 1760–1849* (Cairo: American University in Cairo Press, 1999), 57–58.
47 Bayly, *The Birth of the Modern World*, 12–17.
48 Giorgio Riello and Tirthankar Roy, eds. *How India Clothed the World: The World of South Asian Textiles, 1500–1850* (Leiden: Brill, 2009), 4.
49 Olivier Raveaux, "Spaces and Technologies in the Cotton Industry in the Seventeenth and Eighteenth Centuries: The Example of Printed Calicoes in Marseilles," *Textile History* 36, no. 2 (Nov. 2005): 131–45.
50 Athanasios Gekas, "A Global History of Ottoman Cotton Textiles, 1600–1850," *EUI Working Papers*, No. 2007/30, European University

Institute, Max Weber Programme (San Domenico di Fiesola, Italy: Badia Fiesolana, 2007), 1–12.

51 Sheldon Pollock, "The Cosmopolitan Vernacular," *The Journal of Asian Studies* 57, no. 1 (Feb. 1998): 6–37.

52 Janin Hunt, *The Pursuit of Learning in the Islamic World, 610–2003* (Jefferson, NC: McFarland, 2005), 114.

53 Seema Alavi, "Colonizing the Body?" in *Different Types of History*, ed. Bharati Ray (Delhi: Pearson Education India, 2009), 126–28.

54 Frank, *ReOrient*, 191–95.

55 Kapil Raj, "Colonial Encounters and the Forging of New Knowledge and National Identities: Great Britain and India, 1760–1850." *Osiris*, 2nd ser., 15 (2000): 127–28.

56 Hélène Blais, "Les enquêtes des cartographes en Algérie ou les ambiguïtés de l'usage des savoirs vernaculaires en situation coloniale," *Revue d'histoire moderne et contemporaine* 54, no. 4 (Oct.–Dec. 2007): 70–85.

57 Jean-Marcel Humbert, *L'Égyptomanie: la passion de l'Égypte*. Paris: Les Musées de la ville de Paris, 2000.

58 A.B. Clot Bey, *Aperçu général sur l'Égypte*, vol. 1 (Brussels: Société Belge de Librairies, 1840), 224.

Chapter 2

1 See for instance, J. Brugman, *An Introduction to the History of Modern Arabic Literature in Egypt* (Leiden: Brill, 1984), 8–9; *Modern Arabic Poetry, 1800–1970: The Development of Its Forms and Themes* (Leiden: Brill, 1976), 12, 217.

2 Shawqi Dayf, *Tahrifat al-'amiya li-l-fusha* (Cairo: Dar al-Ma'arif, 1994), 6–7. This book has the merit of having studied in depth the linguistic and grammatical features of the colloquial, but nevertheless, the objective was to point out the correct forms.

3 Madiha Doss, "Réflections sur le début de l'écriture dialectique en Égypte," *Égypte/Monde Arabe* 27–28 (1996): 119–46.

4 Madiha Doss and Humphrey Davies, eds., *al-'Smiya al-misriya al-maktuba* (Cairo: al-Hay'a al-Misriya al-Amma li-l-Kitab, 2013).

5 Sheldon Pollock, "Cosmopolitan and Vernacular in History," *Public Culture* 12, no. 3 (2000) 591–625.

6 Eva Maria Grob, *Documentary Arabic Private and Business Letters on Papyrus* (Berlin: de Gruyter, 2010), 156–58.

7 According to Gladys Franz-Murphy, the word *arsa*, meaning 'open space,' used in some very early contracts, is a word of Coptic origin. See her "A Comparison of the Arabic and Earlier Egyptian Contract Formularies, Part I: The Arabic Contracts from Egypt, 3rd/9th–5th /11th Centuries," *Journal of Near-East Studies* 40, no. 3 (July 1981), 219; as was the word *sharaqi* (land that water did not reach), which was in use many centuries later. See her "Arabic Papyrology and Middle Eastern Studies," *Middle East Studies Association Bulletin* 19, no. 1 (July 1985), 41–42.

8 Ibn Khaldun, *al-Muqaddima* (Beirut: Dar al-Awda, 1981), 464.

9 Werner Diem, *Arabische Privatbriefe des 9. bis 15. Jahrhunderts aus der Österreichischen Nationalbibliothek* (Wiesbaden: Harrassowitz, 1996); Werner Diem, *Arabische amtliche Briefe des 10. bis 16. Jahrhunderts aus der Österreichischen Nationalbibliothek in Wien* (Wiesbaden: Harrassowitz, 1996).

10 Ibn Sudun, *Bringing a Laugh to a Scowling Face: A Study and Critical Edition of the* Nuzhat al-nufus wa-mudhik al-'abus, ed. Arnoud Vrolijk (Leiden: School of Asian, African, and Amerindian Studies, 1998).

11 Eric Geoffroy, "La 'seconde vague': fin XIIIe siècle–XV siècle," in *Les Voies d'Allah: les orders mystiques dans le monde musulman des origins à aujourd'hui*, ed. Alexandre Popovic and Gilles Veinstein (Paris: Fayard, 1996), 55–58.

12 Catherine Mayeur-Jouen and Nicolas Michel, "Cheikhs, *zawiyas* et confréries du Delta central: un paysage religieux autour du XVIe siècle," in *Sociétés rurales ottomanes*, ed. Muhammad Afifi, Rachida Chih, Brigitte Marino, Nicolas Michel, and Isik Tamdogan (Cairo: IFAO, 2005), 139–62.

13 Eric Geoffroy, *Le soufisme en Égypte et en Syrie* (Damascus: Institut français de Damas, 1996), 205–39.

14 Franz Rosenthal, *A History of Muslim Historiography* (Leiden: Brill, 1968), 134–36.

15 Muhammad b. Muhammad Makki, *Tarikh Makka al-Musharaffa* (Beirut: Dal al-Kutub al-Ilmiya, 1997).

16 Donald Little, "Mujir al-Din al-'Ulaymi's Vision of Jerusalem in the Ninth/Fifteenth Century," *Journal of the American Oriental Society* 115, no. 2 (April–July 1995): 237 (author died 1522).

17 Jalal al-Din al-Suyuti, *Husn al-muhadara fi tarikh Misr wa-l-Qahira* (Beirut: Dar al-Kutub al-Ilmiya, 1997).

18 David Morray, *An Ayyubid Notable and His World: Ibn al-Adim and Aleppo as Portrayed in His Biographical Dictionary of People Associated with the City* (Leiden: Brill, 1994).
19 Chase Robinson, *Islamic Historiography* (Cambridge: Cambridge University Press, 2003), 134–40.
20 Noel Coulson, "Muslim Custom and Case Law," *Die Welt des Islam*, n.s. 6, 1, no. 2 (1959): 14–15.
21 Gideon Libson, "On the Development of Custom as a Source of Law in Islamic Law," *Islamic Law and Society* 4, no. 2 (1997): 140–41.
22 Ibn Nujaym, *al-Ashbah wa-l-natha'ir 'ala madhhab Abi Hanifa al-Nu'man* (Beirut: Dar al-Kutub al-Ilmiya, 1985), 104–105; Haim Gerber, *Islamic Law and Culture 1600–1840* (Leiden: Brill, 1999), 105–10; Wael Hallaq, "A Prelude to Ottoman Reform: Ibn Abidin on Custom and Legal Change," in *Histories of the Modern Middle East: New Directions*, ed. Israel Gershoni, Y. Hakan Erdem, and Ursula Wokock (Boulder, CO: Lynne Rienner, 2002), 42–52.
23 Ibn Abidin, *Majmu'at rasa'il Ibn Abidin* (Beirut: Ihya al-Turath al-Arabi), 44–48.
24 Judith Tucker, *In the House of the Law: Gender and Islamic Law in Ottoman Syria and Palestine* (Berkeley: University of California Press, 1998), 16–17.
25 Margaret Larkin, "Popular Poetry in the Post-Classical Period," in *The Cambridge History of Arabic Literature*, vol. 6, *Arabic Literature in the Post-Classical Period*, ed. Roger Allen and D.S. Richards (Cambridge: Cambridge University Press, 2006), 193–94.
26 M.M. Badawi, "Medieval Arabic Drama: Ibn Daniyal," *Journal of Arabic Literature* 13 (1982): 83–107; Li Guo, "Paradise Lost: Ibn Daniyal's Response to Baybar's Campaign against Vice in Cairo," *Journal of the American Oriental Society* 121, no. 2 (April–June 2001): 219–35.
27 Adrian Gully, "Epistles or Grammarians: Illustrations from the *insha* Literature," *British Journal of Middle East Studies* 23, no. 2 (Nov. 1996): 147–48; Maaike Van Berkel, "A Well-mannered Man of Letters or a Cunning Accountant: Qalqashandi and the Historical Position of the *katib*," *Masaq: Islam and the Medieval Mediterranean* 13 (2001): 87–95.
28 John Wansborough, "A Mamluk Letter of 877/1473," *Bulletin of the School of Oriental and African Studies* 24, no. 2 (1961): 200–13.

29 Thomas Bauer, "Mamluk Literature: Misunderstandings and New Approaches," *Mamluk Studies Review* 9, no. 2 (2005): 105–32; Jo Van Steenbergen, "Qalawunid Discourse, Elite Communication and the Mamluk Cultural Matrix: Interpreting a Fourteenth-century Panegyric," *Journal of Arabic Literature* 43, no. 1 (2012): 1–28.

30 Emad Abou Ghazi, "Observations sur la langue à travers l'étude des actes notaires de l'époque mamelouke," *Égypte/Monde Arabe* 27–28 (1996): 147–56.

31 Bruna Soravia, "Les manuels à l'usage des fonctionnaires de l'administration *("Adab al-Katib")* dans l'Islam classique," *Arabica* 52, no. 3 (July 2005): 425–26.

32 Richard Mortel, "The Decline of Mamluk Civil Bureaucracy in the Fifteenth Century: The Career of Abul-Khayr al-Nahhas," *Journal of Islamic Studies* 6, no. 2 (1995): 174; see also Doris Behrens-Abouseif, "Craftsmen, Upstarts and Sufis in the Late Mamluk Period," *Bulletin of the School of Oriental and African Studies* 74, no. 3 (October 2011): 375–95.

33 Gabor Agoston and Bruce Masters, *Encyclopedia of the Ottoman Empire* (New York: Facts on File, 2009), 154.

34 Christine Woodhead, "Reading Ottoman Sehnames: Official Historiography in the Late Sixteenth Century," *Studia Islamica* 104–105 (2007): 67–68.

35 Tarif Khalidi, *Arab Historical Thought in the Classical Period* (Cambridge: Cambridge University Press, 1996), 183–84.

36 Benjamin Lellouch, "Le téléphone arabe au Caire au lendemain de la conquête ottomane: on-dits et rumeurs dans Ibn Iyâs," *Revue du monde musulman et de la Méditerranée* 75–76 (1995): 117–30.

37 Carl Petry, *Protectors or Praetorians: The Last Mamluk Sultans and Egypt's Waning as a Great Power* (Albany: State University of New York Press, 1994), 6–8.

38 Stephan Conermann and Tilman Seindensticker, "Some Remarks on Ibn al-Tawq's (d. 905/1509) Journal, *al-Ta'liq*, vol. 1 (885/1480–890/1485)," *Mamluk Studies Review* 11, no. 2 (2007): 121–35.

39 Dana Sajdi, "A Room of His Own: The 'History' of the Barber of Damascus (fl. 1762)," *MIT Electronic Journal of Middle East Studies* 3 (Fall 2003): 19–35; Muhammad Ibn Kannan al-Salihi, *Yawmiyat shamiya*, ed. Akram Hasan al-'Ulabi (Damascus: Dar al-Tabba', n.d.); Ibn al-Tawq, Shihab al-Din Ahmad, *al-Ta'liq, Yawmiyat Shihab al-Din*

Ahmad Ibn al-Tawq, ed. Shaykh Jaafar al-Muhajir, 3 vols. (Damascus: IFEAD, 2000–2004).

40 Muhammad Ibn Kannan al-Salihi, *Yawmiyat shamiya*, 438, 478.

41 Nelly Hanna, "The Historiography of Ottoman Egypt: History or Entertainment?" in *The Historiography of Islamic Egypt (c. 950–1800)*, ed. Hugh Kennedy (Leiden: Brill, 2001), 237–50.

42 Sheldon Pollock, "The Cosmopolitan Vernacular," *The Journal of Asian Studies* 57, no. 1 (Feb. 1998): 6–37.

43 André Raymond, *Artisans et commerçants*, remains the standard work on the coffee trade passing through Egypt during this period.

44 Peter Gran, *Islamic Roots of Capitalism*, 57–58.

45 Sheldon Pollock, "The Language of Science in Early Modern India," in *Forms of Knowledge in Early Modern Asia*, ed. Sheldon Pollock (Durham, NC: Duke University Press, 2011), 7, 36–37.

46 Shmuel Moreh, *Studies in Modern Arabic Prose and Poetry* (Leiden: Brill, 1987), 63–64.

47 Bruce Masters has written about four such authors in his article, "The View from the Province: Syrian Chronicles of the Eighteenth Century," *Journal of the American Oriental Society* 114, no. 3 (July–Sept. 1994): 353–62.

48 Doris Behrens-Abouseif, "Une polémique anti-ottomane par un artisan au Caire au XVIIe siècle," in *Études sur les villes du Proche-Orient, XVI–XIXe siècles: Hommage à André Raymond*, ed. Brigitte Marino (Damascus: IFEAD, 2001), 55–63.

49 *Al-Damurdashi's Chronicle of Egypt, 1688–1755*, Al-Durra al-Musana fi Akhbar al-Kinana, translated and annotated by Daniel Crecelius and Abd al-Wahhab Bakr (Leiden: Brill, 1991), 8–9.

50 Madiha Doss, "Military Chronicles of Seventeenth-century Egypt as an Aspect of Popular Culture," in *Proceedings of the Colloquium on Logos, Ethos, Mythos in the Middle East and North Africa*, ed. K. Devenyi and T. Ivanyi (Budapest: Eötvös Loránd University Chair for Arabic Studies and Csoma de Kőrős Society, Section of Islamic Studies, 1996), 76.

51 Rachida Chih and Catherine Mayeur-Jouen, "Le soufisme ottoman: Mise en perspective des enjeux historiographiques," in *Le Sufisme à l'époque ottomane*, ed. Rachida Chih and Catherine Mayeur-Jouen (Cairo: IFAO, 2010), 30.

52 Nelly Hanna, "Self Narratives in Arabic Texts 1500–1800," in *The Uses of First Person Writings: Africa, America, Asia, Europe*, ed. François-Joseph Ruggio (Brussels: Peter Lang, 2013), 139–54.

53 Philippe Aries, "Introduction," in *A History of Private Life, Passions of the Renaissance*, trans. from French by Arthur Goldhammer, ed. Roger Chartier (Cambridge, MA: Harvard University Press, 1989), 2–4.

54 Radiy al-Din Yusuf ibn Hanbali, *Bahr al-awam fi-ma asab fihi al-awwam*, ed. Sha'ban Salih (Cairo: Dar al-Thaqafa al-Arabiya, 1990).

55 Ibn Abil-Surur al-Bakri, *al-Muqtadab fima wafaqa lugha ahl Misr min lugha al-'Arab*, ed. Hisham Abdul-Aziz and Adil al-Adawi (Cairo: Akadamiya al-Funun, 2006).

56 Shihab al-Din Ahmad al-Khafaji, *Shifa al-ghalil fima fi kalam al-'Arab min al-dakhil*, ed. Muhamad Abdul Munim Khafaji (Cairo: al-Maktaba al-Azhariya li-l Turath, 2003).

57 Muhammad Amin al-Muhibbi, *Qasd al-sabil fima fi-l-lugha al-'Arabiya min al-dakhil*, 2 vols., ed. 'Uthman Mahmud al-Sini (Riyadh: Maktabat al-Tawba, 1994).

58 Elisabeth Zack, "Colloquial Arabic in the Seventeenth Century: Yusuf al-Magribi's Egyptian Arabic Word-List," in *Approaches to Arabic Dialects*, ed. Martine Haak, Rudolf de Jong, and Kees Versteegh (Leiden: Brill, 2004), 373–90.

59 Nelly Hanna, "The Chronicles of Ottoman Egypt: History or Entertainment?" in *The Historiography of Islamic Egypt (c. 950–1800)*, ed. Hugh Kennedy (Leiden: Brill, 2001), 238.

60 Kamaruzaman Yusoff, "An Overview of the Ms., 'The Paris Fragment,' on the History of Ottoman Egypt in the Seventeenth Century," *Islamic Quarterly* 48, no. 3 (2004): 222–37 and "An Overview of the Ms. '*Zubdat Ikhtisar Tarikh Muluk Misr al-Mahrusa*,'" *Islamic Studies* 41, no. 2 (Summer 2002): 319–33; the linguistic features are discussed on pp. 323–25.

61 Peter Holt, "The Career of Kucuk Muhammad (1676–1694)," *Bulletin of the School of Oriental and African Studies* 26, no. 2 (1963): 270.

62 Peter Holt, "Ottoman Egypt (1517–1798): An Account of Arabic Historical Sources," in *Political and Social Change in Modern Egypt*, ed. P.M. Holt, 3–12 (London: Oxford University Press, 1968), 6.

63 Nagendra Kr. Singh and A. Samiuddin, eds., *Encyclopedic Historiography of the Muslim World*, vol. 1 (Delhi: Global Vision, 2003), 494.

64 Nicolas Michel, "Langues et écritures des papiers publics dans l'Égypte ottoman," *Égypte/Monde Arabe* 27–28 (1996): 148–51.
65 Jon Mandaville, "The Ottoman Court Records of Syria and Jordan," *Journal of the American Oriental Society* 86, no. 3 (July–Sept. 1966): 313.
66 Khaled Sayid Marzuq, ed., *Min watha'iq Bani Suwayf fi-l-'asr al-'uthmani, sijjil min mahkama Bab al-Ali* (Cairo: Dar al-Kutub wa-l-Watha'iq, 2012), 38.
67 Court of Bab Ali, register 129, case 475, dated 1061/1651, 125.
68 Nelly Hanna, "History from Below, Dictionary from Below," in *Innovations in Islam, Traditions and Contributions*, ed. Mehran Kamrava (Los Angeles: University of California Press, 2011), 85–97; Hanna, *In Praise of Books: A Cultural History of Cairo's Middle Class, Sixteenth–Eighteenth Centuries* (Los Angeles: University of California Press, 2003), 129–30.
69 Humphrey Davies, ed., *Yusuf al-Shirbini's* Kitab Hazz al-Quhuf bi-Sharh Qasid Abi Shaduf *(Brains Confounded by the Ode of Abu Shaduf Expounded)*, vol. 1 (Leuven: Peeters, 2005), xxxiii–xxxiv.
70 M. Peled, "Nodding the Necks: A Literary Study of Shirbini's "Hazz al-Quhuf," *Die Welt des Islam*, n.s. 26, nos. 1–4 (1986): 57.
71 Hanna, *In Praise of Books*, 126.
72 al-Jabarti, *'Ajai'b al-athar fi-l-tarajim wa-l-akhbar*, vol. 1, ed. Abdul-Rahim Abdul-Rahman Abdul-Rahim (Cairo: Dar al-Kutub al-Misriya, 1998), 52–55.
73 al-Jabarti, *'Aja'ib al-athar*, vol. 1, 75–76.
74 Some of these letters have survived and will be published by Nasir Ibrahim. He has confirmed to me that the language of these letters makes use of colloquial expressions.
75 Stefan Reichmuth, *The World of Murtada al-Zabidi (1732–91): Life, Networks and Writing* (Oxford: Gibb Memorial Trust, 2009), vii; Rajab Abdul Jawwad Ibrahim, *Lugha al-Amma fi Taj al-Arus* (Cairo: Maktabat al-Adab, 2008).
76 Hanna, *In Praise of Books*, 119.
77 Heikki Palva, "Linguistic Notes on a Dialectical Seventeenth–Eighteenth Century Egyptian Arabic Narrative," *Oriente Moderne* n.s. 80 (2000): 83–97.
78 Febe Armanios, "Christian Copts in Ottoman Egypt: Religious Worldview and Communal Beliefs," PhD diss., The Ohio State University, 2003, 28–36.

79 James Grehan, "The Mysterious Power of Words: Language, Law and Culture in Ottoman Damascus (Seventeenth–Eighteenth Centuries)," *Journal of Social History* (Summer 2004): 995.

80 John Cornelius Baskerville, "From Tahdhiib al-Amma to Tahmiish al-Ammiyya: In Search of Social and Literary Roles for Standard and Colloquial Arabic in Late Nineteenth-century Egypt," PhD diss., University of Texas, 2009, 5–6.

81 Ziad Fahmy, *Ordinary Egyptians: Creating the Modern Nation through Popular Culture* (Palo Alto, CA: Stanford University Press, 2011), 4–7, 39.

82 Baskerville, "From Tahdhiib al-Amma to Tahmiish al-Ammiyya," 155–65.

83 James Lehning, *Peasant and French: Cultural Contact in Rural France during the Nineteenth Century* (Cambridge: Cambridge University Press, 1995), 12–13.

84 Lynda Mugglestone, "The Rise of Received Pronunciation," in *A Companion to the History of the English Language*, ed. Haruko Momma and Michael Matto (Chichester: Blackwell, 2008), 244–45.

Chapter 3

1 Gabriel Baer, "Monopolies and Restrictive Practices of Turkish Guilds," *Journal of the Economic and Social History of the Orient* 13, no. 1 (April 1970): 145–65; Gabriel Baer, *Egyptian Guilds in Modern Times* (Jerusalem: Israel Oriental Society, 1964).

2 Timur Kuran, *The Long Divergence: How Islamic Law Held Back the Middle East* (Princeton, NJ: Princeton University Press, 2011), 132–33, 271.

3 A. Mesud Kucukkalay and Numan Elibol, "Ottoman Imports in the Eighteenth Century: Smyrna (1771–72)," *Middle Eastern Studies* 42, no. 5 (Sept. 2006): 723.

4 Onur Yildirim, "Transformation of the Craft Guilds in Istanbul (1650–1850)," *Islamic Studies* 40, no. 1 (Spring 2001): 49–66; Abdul Karim Rafeq, "Craft Organization, Work Ethics and the Strains of Change in Ottoman Syria," *Journal of the American Oriental Society* 111, no. 3 (July–Sept. 1991): 495–511.

5 Fariba Zarinebaf, "Ottoman Guilds and the State in Eighteenth-century Istanbul," paper presented at the conference "The Rise and Decline of Imperial Leadership," Evanston, IL: Northwestern University, November 2007.

6 Caglar Keydar, "Creation and Destruction of Forms of Manufacturing: The Ottoman Example," in *Between Development and Underdevelopment, 1800–1870*, ed. Jean Batou (Geneva: Center for International Economic History, 1991), 158–61.

7 A. Mesud Kucukkalay, "Imports to Smyrna from 1792 to 1804: New Statistics from the Ottoman Sources," *Journal of the Economic and Social History of the Orient* 51, no. 3 (2008): 487–512.

8 Sevket Pamuk and Jeffrey Williamson, "Ottoman De-industrialization 1800–1913: Assessing the Magnitude, Impact and Response," *The Economic History Review* 64, S1 (Feb. 2011): 159–84.

9 See chapter 2 in this book.

10 Nelly Hanna, *Artisan Entrepreneurs in Cairo and Early Modern Capitalism (1600–1800)*. Syracuse, NY: Syracuse University Press, 15, 58.

11 André Raymond, "Une liste des corporations de métiers au Caire en 1801," *Arabica* 4, no. 2 (May 1957): 154–55.

12 Prasannan Parthasarathi and Giorgio Riello, "Introduction: Cotton Textiles and Global History," in *The Spinning World: A Global History of Cotton Textiles, 1200–1850*, eds. Giorgio Riello and Prasannan Parthasarathi, 1–13 (Oxford: Oxford University Press, 2009).

13 Raymond, *Artisans et commerçants au Caire au XVIIIe* siècle, 2 vols. (Damascus: Institut français de Damas, 1974), 229.

14 Raymond, *Artisans et commerçants*, 229.

15 Court of Bab Ali, register 135, case 1182, p. 303, dated 1027/1617.

16 André Raymond, "Une liste des corporations de métiers au Caire en 1801," 150–63; see also Halil Inalcik, "Capital in the Ottoman Empire," *The Journal of Economic History* 29, no. 1 (March 1969): 104–105.

17 M.P.S. Girard, "Mémoire sur l'agriculture, l'industrie et le commerce de l'Égypte," in *Description de l'Égypte, État Moderne*, vol. 2, no. 1 (Paris: Imprimerie Royale, 1822), 104–13.

18 Girard, "Mémoire," 108–10, 148.

19 Girard, "Mémoire," 193. The destination of these garments is not mentioned by Girard.

20 Stefano Carboni, *Venice and the Islamic World, 828–1979* (Gallimard, France: Metropolitan Museum of Art, 2007), 180–81.

21 Jon Thompson, "Late Mamluk Carpets: Some New Observations," in *The Art of the Mamluks in Egypt and Syria: Evolution and Impact*, ed. Doris Behrens-Abouseif (Bonn: Bonn University Press, 2012), 117.

22 Suraiya Faroqhi, "Declines and Revivals in Textile Production," in *Cambridge History of Turkey: The Later Ottoman Empire, 1603–1839*, vol. 3, ed. Suraiya Faroqhi (Cambridge: Cambridge University Press, 2006), 366.
23 Colette Establet and Jean-Paul Pascual, *Des tissus et des hommes: Damas vers 1700* (Damascus: Institut français du Proche-Orient, 2005), 113–16.
24 Raymond, *Artisans et commerçants*, 130–31.
25 Constantin-François Volney, *Les oeuvres complètes de Volney* (Paris: Didot, 1838), 767; Jacques Peuchet, *Dictionnaire universel de la géographie commerçante*, vol. 5 (Paris: Chez Blanchon, An VIII/1800), 132; Pierre Joseph André Roubaud, *Histoire générale de l'Afrique, de l'Asie et de l'Amérique*, vol. 9 (Paris: Chez des Ventes de la Doue, 1771), 56.
26 Peuchet, *Dictionnaire universel*, 132.
27 Benoît de Maillet, *Description de l'Égypte . . . composée sur les mémoires de M. de Maillet, ancient consul de France au Caire, par M. l'Abbé Le Mascrier* (Paris: Chez Louis Genneau et Jacques Rollin, 1735), 199.
28 Raymond, *Artisans et commerçants*, 130–31; Husam Abdul-Mu'ti, *al-'Ilaqat al-misriya al-hijaziya fi-l-qarn al thamin 'ashar* (Cairo: al-Hay'a al-Misriya al-'Amma li-l-Kitab, Silsila Tarikh al-Misriyin, 1999), 141.
29 F. Vansleb, *The Present State of Egypt or a New Relation of a Late Voyage into that Kingdom Performed in the Years 1672 and 1673* (originally printed London: R.E. John Starkey, 1678, repr. Westmead: Gregg International Publishers, 1972), 123–24; see also Raymond, *Artisans et commerçants*, 180–82.
30 Girard, "Mémoire," 186.
31 Sahar Ali Hanafi Ali Khalil, "al-'Ilaqat al-tujariya bayn Misr wa Bilad al-Sham al-Kubra fi-l-qarn al-thamin ashar," PhD diss., Cairo University, Faculty of Arts, 1998, 160–64.
32 Establet and Pascual, *Des tissus et des hommes*, 198.
33 Constantin-François Volney, *Travels through Syria and Egypt in the Years 1783, 1784, and 1785*, 2 vols. (repub. Westmead: Gregg International, 1972), 228.
34 Volney, *Travels through Syria and Egypt*, 228; Establet and Pascual, *Des tissus et des hommes*, 198. In a recent publication Prasannan Parthasarathi noted that cotton cloth was exported from India to the Caribbean to clothe the slaves working in plantations there. See Prasannan Parthasarathi, *Why Europe Grew Rich and Asia Did Not: Global Economic Divergence, 1600–1850* (New York: Cambridge

University Press, 2011), 25–26; on this subject see also Willis, "European Consumption and Asian Production in the Seventeenth and Eighteenth Century," in *Consumption and the World of Goods*, ed. John Brewer and Roy Porter (London: Routledge, 1993), 136.

35 M. Champon, *Le Commerce de l'Amérique par Marseilles*, vol. 2 (Avignon, 1764), 391.

36 Edhem Eldem, "French Trade and Commercial Policy in the Levant in the Eighteenth Century," *Oriente Moderne Nuova Serie* 18, no. 79 (1999): 31–32.

37 Raymond, *Artisans et commerçants*, 180–82.

38 Girard, "Mémoire," 186, 193.

39 Raymond, *Artisans et commerçants*, 103–104.

40 Jan de Vries, "The Industrial Revolution and the Industrious Revolution," *The Journal of Economic History* 54, no. 2 (June 1994): 249–70.

41 John Chalcraft, "The End of Guilds in Egypt: Restructuring Textiles in the Long Nineteenth Century," in *Crafts and Craftsmen of the Middle East: Fashioning the Individual in the Muslim Mediterranean*, ed. Randi Deguilhem and Suraiya Faroqhi (London: I.B.Tauris, 2005), 344–46.

42 Naser Uthman, "La production textile à Rosette au XVIIIe siècle," *Rives Méditerranéennes* 29 (2008): 2–11.

43 Parthasarathi and Riello, "Introduction," 1–7.

44 Husam Abdul-Mu'ti, "Sina'a al-aqmisha fi Misr khilal 'asr al-'uthmani, 1517–1817," *al-Ruznama* 4 (2006): 330–33.

45 Raymond, *Artisans et commerçants*, 182.

46 BA 191, case 326, dated 16 Safar 1121/1709. The text of this case was published by Salwa Ali Milad, *al-Watha'iq al-'uthmaniya, dirasa arshifiya watha'iqiya li-sijillat mahkama al-Bab al-'Ali*, vol. 2 (Alexandria: Dar al-Thaqafa al-Ilmiya, 2000), 496–97.

47 Husam Abdul-Mu'ti, "Sinaa al-aqmisha," 341–42.

48 Establet and Pascual, *Des tissus et des hommes*, 202–206.

49 Olivier Raveaux, "Spaces and Technologies in the Cotton Industry in the Seventeenth and Eighteenth Centuries: The Example of Printed Calicoes in Marseilles," *Textile History* 36, no. 2 (Nov. 2005).

50 Bethany J. Walker, "Rethinking Mamluk Textiles," *Mamluk Studies Review* 4 (2000): 186.

51 Court of Salihiya Najmiya, register 531, case 258, dated 1194/1780, pp. 197–98.

52 Jomard, "Description de la ville et de la citadelle du Kaire," *Paris: Description de l'Égypte, État Moderne* 1, 2nd ed. Vol. 18, pt. 2 (1829), 411.
53 Michelle Maskiell, "Consuming Kashmir: Shawls and Empire, 1500–2000," *Journal of World History* 13, no. 1 (Spring 2002): 39.
54 Stéphane Flachat, *L'industrie: Recueil des traités élémentaires sur l'industrie française et étrangère* (Paris: Tenre et Dupuy, imprimeurs-éditeurs, 1834), 136.
55 Jean-Claude Flachat, *Observations sur le commerce et sur les arts*, vol. 2 (Lyon: Chez Jacuenod père et Rusand, 1766), 270; Colette Establet et Jean-Paul Pascual, "Les tissus dans les boutiques, les tissus dans les maisons: Damas vers 1700," *Rives nord-méditerrannéenes* 29 (2008): 18.
56 Carboni, *Venice and the Islamic World*, 183, 323–24.
57 Court of al-Zahid, register 693, case 266, dated 1148/1735, p. 119.
58 David Landes, *The Unbound Prometheus: Technological Change and Industrial Development in Western Europe from 1750 to the Present* (London: Cambridge University Press, 1969), 148–49.
59 Liliane Hilaire-Perez, "Transferts technologiques, droit et territories: le cas franco-anglais au XVIIIe siècle" *Revue d'histoire moderne et contemporaine* 44, no. 4 (Oct.–Dec. 1997): 549.
60 Joseph Fletcher, "Integrative History: Parallels and Interconnections in the Early Modern Period, 1500–1800," *Journal of Turkish Studies* 9 (1985): 37–57.
61 See chapter 4 in this book.
62 Giorgio Riello, "The Globalization of Cotton Textiles: Indian Cottons, Europe, and the Atlantic World, 1600–1850," in *The Spinning World: A Global History of Cotton Textiles, 1200–1850*, eds. Giorgio Riello and Prasannan Parthasarathi, 261–87 (Oxford: Oxford University Press, 2009), 276.
63 Abdul-Mu'ti, "Sina'a al-aqmisha," 346.
64 Milad, *al-Watha'iq al-'uthmaniyya*, vol. 2, 496–97.
65 Uthman, "La production textile à Rosette," 3.
66 Abdul-Mu'ti, "Sina'a al-aqmisha," 346.
67 Hanna, *Artisan Entrepreneurs*, 180–84; Court of Salihiya Najmiya 531, case 258 (1194/1780), 197–98.
68 Mackie, "Towards an Understanding of Mamluk Silks: National and International Considerations," *Muqarnas* 2 (1984): 127.
69 Mackie, "Towards an Understanding of Mamluk Silks," 127–46; Patricia Baker, *Islamic Textiles* (London: British Museum Press, 1995),

152; John Gillow, *Textiles of the Islamic World* (London: Thames and Hudson, 2010), 18.

Chapter 4

1 Zaheer Baber, *The Science of Empire: Scientific Knowledge, Civilization and Colonial Rule in India* (Albany: State University of New York Press, 1996), 9–10.

2 Roshdi Rashed, *The Development of Arabic Mathematics: Between Arithmetic and Algebra* (Dordrecht, Netherlands: Kluwer Academic Publishers, 1994); George Saliba, *Islamic Science and the Making of the Renaissance* (Cambridge, MA: MIT Press, 2007).

3 Toby E. Huff, *The Rise of Early Modern Science: Islam, China, and the West*, 2nd ed. (Cambridge: Cambridge University Press, 1993, 2003), 47.

4 David Landes, *Prometheus Unbound: Technological Change and Industrial Development in Western Europe from 1750 to the Present* (Cambridge: Cambridge University Press, 2003), 28.

5 H. Floris Cohen, "Review Essay," in "From West to East, from East to West? Early Science between Civilizations," *Early Science and Medicine* 17 (2012): 339–50, shows that this view continues to be largely prevalent in the literature.

6 Emilie Savage-Smith, "Islam," in *The Cambridge History of Science*, vol. 4, *Eighteenth Century Science*, ed. Roy Porter (Cambridge: Cambridge University Press, 2003), 659–61.

7 William Gervase Clarence-Smith, "Technological and Scientific Change in Early Modern Islam, 1450–1850," paper given at the XIV International Economic History Congress, Helsinki, 2006.

8 Peter Gran, *Islamic Roots of Capitalism: Egypt 1760–1840* (Cairo: American University in Cairo Press, 1999), 170; Sabri al-Adl, "The Study of Astronomy According to the Chronicle of al-Jabarti," in *Society and Economy in Egypt and the Eastern Mediterranean, 1600–1900, Essays in Honour of André Raymond*, ed. Nelly Hanna and Raouf Abbas (Cairo: American University in Cairo Press, 2005), 181–200; Raimer Broemer, "Scientific Practice, Patronage, Salons and Enterprise in Eighteenth-century Cairo: Examination of al-Gabarti's History of Egypt," in *Multicultural Science in the Ottoman Empire*, ed. Ekmeleddin Ihsanoglu, Kostas Chatzis, and Efthymios Nicolaidis (Turnhout, Belgium: Brepols, 2003), 107–20.

9 Avner Ben Zaken, *Cross-Cultural Scientific Exchanges in the Eastern Mediterranean, 1560–1660* (Baltimore: Johns Hopkins University Press, 2010).

10 James M. Blaut, "Diffusionism: A Uniformitarian Critique," *Annals of the Association of American Geographers* 77, no. 1 (March 1987): 30–47.

11 Romain Bertrand, *L'Histoire à parts égales: Récits d'une rencontre Orient–Occident (XVIe–XVIIe siècle)* (Paris: Editions du Seuil, 2011), 12–14, 59, 68–84.

12 Andrés I. Pireto, *Missionary Scientists: Jesuit Science in Spanish South America, 1570–1810* (Nashville, TN: Vanderbilt University Press, 2011), 2, 82.

13 Athanasios Gekas, "A Global History of Ottoman Cotton Textiles, 1600–1850," *EUI Working Papers*, No. 2007/30, European University Institute, Badia Fiesolana (2007), 1–23; Olivier Raveaux, "Spaces and Technologies in the Cotton Industry in the Seventeenth and Eighteenth Centuries: The Example of Printed Calicoes in Marseilles," *Textile History* 36, no. 2 (Nov. 2005): 131–45; Olivier Raveaux, "The Birth of the Calico Printing in Europe: The Case of Marseilles (1648–1692)," paper presented at the GEHN conference, "Global Histories of Economic Development: Cotton Textiles and Other Global Industries in the Early Modern Period," Fondation Les Treilles, March 2006; Liliane Hilaire-Pérez, "Cultures techniques et pratiques de l'échange, entre Lyon et le Levant: inventions et réseaux au XVIIIe siècle," *Revue d'histoire moderne et contemporaine* 49, no. 1 (2002): 89–114.

14 *Abd al-Rahman al-Jabarti's History of Egypt, Ajaib al-Athar fi'l Tarajim wa'l-Akhbar*, ed. Thomas Philipp and Moshe Perlmann (Stuttgart: Franz Steiner Verlag, 1994), vol. 1, 664–65.

15 Clifford D. Connor, *A People's History of Science: Miners, Midwives and "Low Mechanicks"* (New York: Nation Books, 2005), 249–50.

16 Jean-Claude Flachat, *Observations sur le commerce et sur les arts*, vol. 1 (Lyon: Chez Jacquenod père et Rusand, 1766), 7.

17 "Mémoire sur l'ophthalmie endémique en Égypte," in *Description de l'Égypte*, vol. 13, *État Moderne*, 2nd ed. (Paris: Panckoucke, 1823), 36–50.

18 "Notice sur l'ophtalmie régnante par le citoyen Bruant, médecin ordinaire de l'armée," in *La Décade Égyptienne*, vol. 1 (An VII/1799), p. 63.

19 Salvatore Furnari, *Traité pratique des maladies des yeux* (Paris: Chez J-B. Bailliere, 1841), 139–43.

20 Catherine Kelly, "Medicine and the Egyptian Campaign: The Development of the Military Medical Officer during the Napoleonic Wars c. 1798–1801," *Canadian Bulletin of Medical History* 27, no. 2 (2010), 337.

21 See chapter 3 in this book.

22 Abdul-Mu'ti, "Sinaa al-aqmisha," 341.

23 Mireille Lobligeois, "Ateliers publics et filatures privées à Pondichéry après 1816," *Bulletin de l'École française d'Extrême Orient* 59 (1972): 11–12, 15–22.

24 Benoît de Maillet, *Description de l'Égypte . . . composée sur les mémoires de M. de Maillet, ancien consul de France au Caire, par M. l'Abbé Le Mascrier* (Paris: Chez Louis Genneau et Jacques Rollin, 1735), 191.

25 Edmé François Jomard, "Description de la ville et de la citadelle du Kaire," in *Description de l'Égypte, État Moderne*, vol. 1 (Paris: Imprimerie Panckoucke, 1829), 383–84.

26 Vivant Denon, *Voyage dans la basse et haute Égypte pendant les campagnes du général Bonaparte* (Paris: Imprimerie Didot l'Aîné, An X/1801), 64.

27 Charles Sigisbert Sonnini, *Voyage dans la Haute et Basse Égypte*, vol. 1 (Paris: F. Buisson, An VII/1799), 360.

28 Jean-Gabriel Peltier, *Paris pendant l'année 1800*, vol. 28 (London: Imprimerie T. Baylis, 1800), 224–25.

29 Beverly Lemire and Giorgio Riello, "Textile and Fashion in Early Modern Europe," *Journal of Social History* 41, no. 1 (2008): 887–916.

30 Susan Fairlie, "Dyestuffs in the Eighteenth Century," *Economic History Review*, n.s., 17, no. 3 (1965): 489–91.

31 M. Scheffer, *Essai sur l'art de la teinture* (Paris: Chez Goeury, 1803), 124–25.

32 Pierre-Simon Girard, "Mémoire sur l'agriculture, l'industrie et le commerce de l'Égypte," in *Description de l'Égypte, État Moderne*, 2, no. 1 (Paris: Panckoucke, 1812), 111.

33 Abdul-Karim Rafeq, "The Economic Organization of Cities in Ottoman Syria," in *The Urban Social History of the Middle East, 1750–1950*, ed. Peter Sluglett (Syracuse, NY: Syracuse University Press, 2008), 109.

34 Court of Bab Ali, register no. 123, Hujja no. 1055, dated 1056, case no. 100, p. 18.

35 Frederic Hasselquist, *Voyage dans le Levant dans les années 1749, 1750, 1751, et 1752* (Paris: Chez Saugrain le Jeune, 1769), 161.

36 Jean-Antoine-Claude Chaptal, *Chimie appliquée aux arts*, vol. 4 (Paris: Imprimerie de Crapelet, 1807), 167–75. There is today a *lycée* in Paris that bears his name. Sal ammoniac had many other uses.

37 Beaulieu, *L'art de peindre et d'imprimer les toiles en grand et en petit teints* (Paris: Chez Goeury, An VIII/1800), 12–17.

38 Chaptal, *Chimie appliquée aux arts*, 426–27.

39 Jean-Baptiste Dumas, *Précis de l'art de la teinture* (Paris: Bechet Jeune, 1846), 58.

40 Abdul-Mu'ti, "Sina'a al-aqmisha," 341.

41 Jean de Thevenot, *Suite du Voyage de M. de Thevenot au Levant*, second part (Paris: Chez Charles Angot, 1689), 115–18.

42 Constantin-François Volney, *Voyage en Égypte et en Syrie pendant les années 1783, 1784, et 1785*, vol. 2 (Paris: Parmantier, 1825), 145.

43 Jean-Élie Bertrand, *Description des arts et métiers*, vol. 3 (Neuchâtel: Imprimerie de la Société typographyque, 1775), 419–20; M. Granger, *Relation du Voyage en Égypte par le Sieur Granger fait en 1730* (Paris: Chez Jacques Vincent, 1745). His description of how sal ammoniac was made is on pages 250–56.

44 Le Pileur d'Appligny, *L'art de la teinture des fils et des étoffes de coton précédé d'une théorie* (Paris: Chez Moutard, Libraire de la Reine, Quai des Augustins, 1776), 145.

45 *Bulletin de la Société pour l'encouragement de l'industrie nationale* (Paris: Chez Madame Huzard, An X/1802), 142.

46 J.-Cl. Delametherie, *Journal de physique, de chimie, d'histoire naturelle et des arts*, vol. 51 (Paris: Chez Fuchs, 1800), 307.

47 Pierre-Joseph Macquer, *Dictionnaire de Chimie contenant la Théorie et la Pratique de cette science*, vol. 1 (Paris: Imprimerie de Monsieur, 1778), 110.

48 Girard, *Mémoires*, 122.

49 Girard, *Mémoires*, 123.

50 *Lettres édifiantes et curieuses écrites des missions étrangères*, vol. 3, in *Mémoire du Levant* (Lyon: Chez J. Vernarel et Etienne Cabin, 1819), 420–21.

51 François Crouzet, "France," in *The Industrial Revolution in National Context: Europe and the USA*, ed. Mukilas Teich and Roy Porter (Cambridge: Cambridge University Press, 1996), 37.

52 Chaptal, *Chimie appliquée*, 169–70.

53 Susan Lowengard, *The Creation of Color in Eighteenth-Century Europe* (New York: Columbia University Press, 2006): 19, www.e-gutenberg-e.org/lowengard
54 Susan Lowengard, "Colors and Color-Making in the Eighteenth Century," in *Consumers and Luxury: Consumer Culture in Europe, 1650–1850*, ed. Maxine Berg and Helen Clifford (Manchester, UK: Manchester University Press, 1999), 104–105.
55 Olga Katsiardi-Hering, "The Allure of Red Cotton Yarn and How It Came to Vienna: Associations of Greek Artisans and Merchants Operating between the Ottoman and the Hapsburg Empires," in *Merchants in the Ottoman Empire*, ed. Suraiya Faroqhi and Gilles Veinstein (Paris and Louvain: Peeters, 2008), 97–131.
56 Hilaire-Perez, "Cultures techniques et pratiques."
57 David Landes, *The Unbound Prometheus: Technological Change and Industrial Development in Western Europe from 1750 to the Present* (Cambridge: Cambridge University Press, 1969), 148–49.
58 Liliane Hilaire-Perez, "Transferts technologiques, droit et territoires: le cas franco-anglais au XVIIIe siècle," *Revue d'histoire moderne et contemporaine* 44, no. 4 (Oct.–Dec. 1997): 547–79.
59 A.B. Clot Bey, *Aperçu général sur l'Égypte*, vol. 2 (Brussels: Haumon et Cie, 1840), 225–26.
60 Auguste Colin, "Lettres sur l'Égypte: Industries manufacturières," *Revue des Deux Mondes* 14, no. 4 (1838): 528.
61 *Dictionnaire chronologique et raisonné des découvertes en France de 1789 à la fin de 1820*, vol. 4 (Paris: Chez Louis Colas, 1822), 99.
62 Monsieur Blanchi et al., *Dictionnaire du commerce et des marchandises contenant tout ce qui concerne le commerce de terre et de mer*, vol. 2 (Paris: Guillaumin et Cie, 1839), 1956.
63 Jean-Baptiste Dumas, *Traité de chimie appliquée aux arts*, vol. 8 (Paris: Imprimerie Alexandre Bailly, 1846), 401.
64 Johann Carl Leuchs, *Traité complet des propriétés, de la préparation et de l'emploi des matières tinctoriales et des couleurs* (Paris: Imprimerie Fournier, 1829), 286.
65 Pierre Jaubert, *Dictionnaire raisonné universel des arts et des métiers*, vol. 4 (Lyon: Chez Amable Leroy, 1801), 262.
66 Girard, *Mémoires*, 186.
67 *Arrêt du Conseil d'État du Roi qui accorde divers privilèges et exemptions*

à la manufacture royale de Saint Chaumond, 21 décembre 1756 (Lyon: Imprimerie P. Valfray, Imprimeur du roi, 1757).

68 René Tresse, "Le Conservatoire des Arts et Métiers et la Société d'encouragement de l'industrie nationale au debut du XIX siècle," in *Revue d'histoire des sciences et de leurs applications* 5, no. 5, 3 (1952): 252–53.

69 Louis Baillot, *Nouveau Manuel du Teinturier* (Paris: Bachelier Libraire, 1819).

70 J.B. Vitalis, *Manuel du Teinturier sur filé et sur coton filé* (Rouen: Chez Megard, 1810).

71 Alfred Labouchère, *Oberkampf 1738–1815* (Paris: Librairie Hachette, 1866), 139.

72 Agusti Nieto-Galan, "Between Craft Routines and Academic Rules: Natural Dyestuffs and the 'Art' of Dyeing in the Eighteenth Century," in *Materials and Expertise in Early Modern Europe: Between Market and Laboratory*, ed. Ursula Klein and E.C. Spary, 321–53 (Chicago: University of Chicago Press, 2010), 324n11; France, Office national de la propriété industrielle, *Description des machines et procédés consignés dans les brevets*, vol. 29 (Paris: Chez Madame Huzard, 1836), 423.

73 Descotils et Berthollet, "Observations sur les qualités tinctoriales du henneh," in *La Décade Égyptienne*, vol. 2 (An VIII/1800), 164–66.

74 France, Ministère du commerce et de l'agriculture: Office national de la propriété industrielle, *Descriptions des machines et des procédés pour lesquels des brevets d'invention ont été pris sous le régime de la loi du 5 juillet 1844*, vol. 69 (Paris: Imprimerie imperiale, 1870), 34.

75 Louis Piesse, *Itinéraire historique et descriptif de l'Algérie, comprenant le Tell et le Sahara* (Paris: Imprimerie de Ch. Lahure, 1862), LX.

76 Alfred Labouchère, *Oberkampf, 1738–1815* (Paris: Librairie Hachette, 1866), 39.

77 Société des gens de lettres, *Nouvel esprit des journaux français et étrangers*, vol. 12 (Brussels: Imprimerie de Weissenbruch, 1804), 156.

78 Jack Goody, *The Theft of History* (Cambridge: Cambridge University Press, 2008).

79 Jean-Pierre-Marie Dana, "Observations sur la préparation du carthame, ou safron bâtard, nommé le *linnée carthamus tinctirius*," *Mémoire de l'Académie de Science à Turin, Année 1792 à 1800*, vol. 6 (Turin: Imprimerie nationale, 1801), 157.

80 Roland de la Platière, *Encyclopédie méthodique: manufactures, arts et métiers*, vol. 1 (Paris: Panckoucke, 1785), 218.

81 Societe Montyon et Franklin, *Portraits et histoire des Hommes Utiles*, vol. 1 (Paris: Lebrun Libraire Éditeur, 1841).

82 R. O'Reilly, *Essai sur le blanchiment, avec la description de la nouvelle méthode* (Paris: Chez Deterville, An IX/1801), 132; Chaptal, *Chimie appliquée*, vol. 4, 426.

83 Louis Figuier, *Les Merveilles de l'Industrie* (Paris: Furne, Jouvet et Cie, 1860), 509–10.

84 William Nicholson, ed., *Journal of Natural Philosophy, Chemistry and the Arts*, vol. 4 printed for the author (London: Stratford, Crowncourt, and Temple Bar, 1801), 470.

85 Pamela O. Long, *Artisan/Practitioners and the Rise of the New Sciences, 1400–1600* (Corvallis, OR: Oregon State University Press, 2011); Pamela Smith, *The Body of the Artisan: Art and Experience in the Scientific Revolution* (Chicago: University of Chicago Press, 2004); Connor, *A People's History of Science*.

86 James A. Secord, "Knowledge in Transit," *Isis* 95, no. 4 (Dec. 2004): 657–58.

87 E.P. Thompson, *The Making of the English Working Class* (New York: Pantheon Books, 1964), 831.

88 Vincent Ilardi, *Renaissance Vision from Spectacles to Telescopes* (Philadelphia: American Philosophical Society, 2007), 250–51.

89 David Washbrook, "From Comparative Sociology to Global History: Britain and India in the Pre-history of Modernity," *Journal of the Economic and Social History of the Orient* 40, no. 4 (1997): 410–43.

90 David Washbrook, "A Global History of Modernity: A Response to a Reply," *Journal of the Economic and Social History of the Orient* 41, no. 3 (1998): 300.

Bibliography

Archival Sources: Court Records of Cairo

Court of Bab Ali: registers 119, 123, 129, 135

Court of Salihiya Najmiya: register 531

Court of al-Zahid: register 693

Primary Sources

Bulletin de la Société pour l'encouragement de l'industrie nationale. Paris: Chez Madame Huzard, An X/1802.

Dictionnaire chronologique et raisonné des découvertes en France de 1789 à la fin de 1820. Vol. 4. Paris: Chez Louis Colas, 1822.

France, Ministère du commerce et de l'agriculture. Office national de la propriété industrielle. *Description des machines et procédés consignés dans les brevets*. Vol. 29. Paris: Chez Madame Huzard, 1836.

France, Ministère du commerce et de l'agriculture. Office national de la propriété industrielle. *Descriptions des machines et des procédés pour lesquels des brevets d'invention ont été pris sous le régime de la loi du 5 juillet 1844*. Vol. 69. Paris: Imprimerie Impériale, 1870.

Lettres édifiantes et curieuses écrites des missions étrangères écrites par des missionaires. Vol. 3. In *Mémoire du Levant*. Lyon: Chez J. Vernarel et Étienne Cabin, 1819.

"Notice sur l'ophtalmie régnante par le citoyen Bruant, médecin ordinaire de l'armée." *La Décade Égyptienne*. Vol. 1, An VII/1799, 58–63.

Société des gens de lettres. *Nouvel esprit des journaux français et étrangers*. Vol. 12. Brussels: Imprimerie de Weissenbruch, 1804.

Société Montyon et Franklin. *Portraits et histoire des Hommes Utiles*. Vol. 1. Paris: Lebrun Libraire Éditeur, 1841.

Secondary Sources

Abdul Jawwad Ibrahim, Rajab. *Lugha al-Amma fi Taj al-'arus*. Cairo: Maktabat al-Adab, 2008.

Abdul-Mu'ti, Husam. *Al-'ilaqat al-misriya al-higaziya fi-l qarn al-thamin 'ashar*. Cairo: al-Hay'a al-Misriya al-'Amma li-l-Kitab, Silsila Tarikh al-Misriyin, 1999.

———. "Sina'a al-aqmisha fi Misr khilal al-'asr al-'uthmani, 1517–1817." *al-Ruznama* 4 (2006): 305–73.

Abou-El-Haj, Rifaat. *Formation of the Modern State, The Ottoman Empire: Sixteenth to Eighteenth Centuries*. Albany, NY: State University of New York Press, 1991.

Abou Ghazi, Emad. "Observations sur la langue à travers l'étude des actes notaires de l'époque mamelouke." *Égypte/Monde Arabe* 27–28 (1996): 147–56.

Adas, Michael. "Contested Hegemony: The Great War and the Afro-Asian Assault on the Civilizing Mission Ideology." *Journal of World History* 15, no. 1 (March 2004): 31–63.

al-Adl, Sabri. "The Study of Astronomy According to the Chronicle of al-Jabarti." In *Society and Economy in Egypt and the Eastern Mediterranean, 1600–1900: Essays in Honour of André Raymond*, edited by Nelly Hanna and Raouf Abbas, 181–200. Cairo: American University in Cairo Press, 2005.

Agoston, Gabor, and Bruce Masters. *Encyclopedia of the Ottoman Empire*. New York: Facts on File, 2009.

Alavi, Seema. "Colonizing the Body?" In *Different Types of History*, edited by Bharati Ray, 126–28. Delhi: Pearson Education India, 2012.

Amin, Samir. "Colonialism and the Rise of Capitalism: A Comment." *Science & Society* 54, no. 1 (Spring 1990): 67–72.

———. *Global History: A View from the South*. Cape Town: Pambazuka Press, 2011.

Aries, Philippe. "Introduction." In *A History of Private Life, Passions of the Renaissance*, translated from French by Arthur Goldhammer, edited by Roger Chartier, 1–11. Cambridge, MA: Harvard University Press, 1989.

Armanios, Febe. "Christian Copts in Ottoman Egypt: Religious Worldview and Communal Beliefs." PhD diss., The Ohio State University, 2003.

Arrêt du Conseil d'État du Roi qui accorde divers privilèges et exemptions à la manufacture royale de Saint Chaumond, 21 décembre 1756. Lyon: Imprimerie P. Valfray, Imprimeur du roi, 1757.

Ashmawi, Sayyid. "*al-Muqawama bi-hila fi Misr al-'uthmaniya.*" In *Al-rafd wa-l-ihtijaj fi-l-mujtama al-misri fi-l-'asr al-'uthmani*, edited by Nasir Ibrahim, 137–70. Cairo: Markaz al-Buhuth wa-l-Dirasat al-Ijtima'iya, 2004.

Baber, Zaheer. *The Science of Empire: Scientific Knowledge, Civilization and Colonial Rule in India*. Albany: State University of New York Press, 1996.

Badawi, M.M. "Medieval Arabic Drama: Ibn Daniyal." *Journal of Arabic Literature* 13 (1982): 83–107.

Baer, Gabriel. *Egyptian Guilds in Modern Times*. Jerusalem: Israel Oriental Society, 1964.

———. "Monopolies and Restrictive Practices of Turkish Guilds." *Journal of the Economic and Social History of the Orient* 13, no. 1 (April 1970): 145–65.

———. "The Waqf as a Prop for the Social System (Sixteenth to Twentieth Centuries)." *Islamic Law and Society* 4, no. 3 (1997): 264–97.

Baillot, Louis. *Nouveau Manuel du Teinturier*. Paris: Bachelier Libraire, 1819.

Baker, Patricia L. *Islamic Textiles*. London: British Museum Press, 1995.

al-Bakri, Ibn Abil-Surur. *al-Muqtadab fima wafaqa lugha ahl Misr min lugha al-'arab*, edited by Hisham Abdul-Aziz and Adil al-Adawi. Cairo: Akadamiya al-Funun, 2006.

Barendse, R.J. *The Arabian Sea: The Indian Ocean World of the Seventeenth Century*. New York: Sharpe Inc., 2002.

Baskerville, John Cornelius. "From Tahdhiib al-Amma to Tahmiish al-Ammiyya: In Search of Social and Literary Roles for Standard and Colloquial Arabic in Late Nineteenth-century Egypt." PhD diss., University of Texas, 2009.

Bauer, Thomas. "Mamluk Literature: Misunderstandings and New Approaches." *Mamluk Studies Review* 9, no. 2 (2005): 105–32.

Bayly, Christopher A. *The Birth of the Modern World, 1780–1914*. Oxford: Blackwell, 2004.

Beaulieu (spécialiste des toiles peintes). *L'art de peindre et d'imprimer les toiles en grand et en petit teints*. Paris: Chez Goeury, An VIII/1800.

Behrens-Abouseif, Doris. "Craftsmen, Upstarts and Sufis in the Late Mamluk Period." *Bulletin of the School of Oriental and African Studies* 74, no. 3 (October 2011): 375–95.

———. "Une polémique anti-ottomane par un artisan au Caire au XVIIe siècle." In *Études sur les villes du Proche-Orient, XVI–XIXe siècles: Hommage à André Raymond*, edited by Brigitte Marino, 55–63. Damascus: IFEAD, 2001.

Ben Zaken, Avner. *Cross-Cultural Scientific Exchanges in the Eastern Mediterranean, 1560–1660.* Baltimore: Johns Hopkins University Press, 2010.

Berg, Maxine. *The Age of Manufactures, 1700–1820: Industry, Innovation and Work in Britain.* 2nd ed. London: Taylor and Francis Library, 2005.

Bertrand, Jean-Élie. *Description des arts et métiers.* Vol. 3. Neuchâtel: Imprimerie de la Société typographyque, 1775.

Bertrand, Romain. *L'Histoire à parts égales: Récits d'une rencontre Orient–Occident (XVIe–XVIIe siècle).* Paris: Editions du Seuil, 2011.

Blais, Hélène. "Les enquêtes des cartographes en Algérie ou les *ambigüités* de l'usage des savoirs vernaculaires en situation colonial." *Revue d'histoire moderne et contemporaine* 54, no. 4 (Oct.–Dec. 2007): 70–85.

Blanchi, Monsieur, et al. *Dictionnaire du commerce et des marchandises contenant tout ce qui concerne le commerce de terre et de mer.* Vol. 2. Paris: Guillaumin et Cie, 1839.

Blanqui, Adolphe-Jérôme. *Dictionnaire du commerce et de l'industrie.* Vol. 1. Brussels: Imprimerie A. Cauvin, 1837.

Blaut, James M. "Diffusionism: A Uniformitarian Critique." *Annals of the Association of American Geographers* 77, no. 1 (March 1987): 30–47.

Braudel, Fernand. *The Mediterranean and the Mediterranean World in the Age of Philip II.* Vol. 2. Translated by Sian Reynolds. Berkeley: University of California Press, 1995.

Broemer, Raimer. "Scientific Practice, Patronage, Salons and Enterprise in Eighteenth-century Cairo: Examination of al-Gabarti's History of Egypt." In *Multicultural Science in the Ottoman Empire*, edited by Ekmeleddin Ihsanoglu, Kostas Chatzis, and Efthymios Nicolaidis, 107–20. Turnhout, Belgium: Brepols, 2003.

Brugman, J. *An Introduction to the History of Modern Arabic Literature in Egypt.* Leiden: Brill, 1984.

———. *Modern Arabic Poetry, 1800–1970: The Development of Its Forms and Themes.* Leiden: Brill, 1976.

Bulut, Mehmet. "The Role of the Ottomans and the Dutch in the Commercial Integration between the Levant and the Atlantic in the Seventeenth Century." *Journal of the Economic and Social History of the Orient* 45, no. 2 (2002): 197–230.

Burrows, Mathews. "*Mission Civilisatrice*: French Cultural Policy in the Middle East, 1860–1914." *The Historical Journal* 29, no. 1 (1986): 109–35.

Carboni, Stefano. *Venice and the Islamic World, 828–1979*. Gallimard, France: Metropolitan Museum of Art, 2007.

Casale, Giancarlo. *The Ottoman Age of Exploration*. New York: Oxford University Press, 2010.

Chalcraft, John. "The End of Guilds in Egypt: Restructuring Textiles in the Long Nineteenth Century." In *Crafts and Craftsmen of the Middle East: Fashioning the Individual in the Muslim Mediterranean*, edited by Randi Deguilhem and Suraiya Faroqhi, 338–67. London: I.B.Tauris, 2005.

Champon, M. *Le Commerce de l'Amérique par Marseilles*. Vol. 2. Avignon, 1764.

Chaptal, Jean-Antoine-Claude. *Chimie appliquée aux arts*. Vol. 4. Paris: Imprimerie de Crapelet, 1807.

Chih, Rachida, and Catherine Mayeur-Jouen. "Le soufisme ottoman: Mise en perspective des enjeux historiographiques." In *Le Sufisme à l'époque ottomane*, edited by Rachida Chih and Catherine Mayeur-Jouen, 1–55. Cairo: IFAO, 2010.

Clot Bey, A.B. *Aperçu général sur l'Égypte*. Vol. 1. Brussels: Société Belge de Librairies, 1840.

———. *Aperçu général sur l'Égypte*. Vol. 2. Brussels: Haumon et Cie., 1840.

Cohen, Amnon. *The Guilds of Ottoman Jerusalem*. Leiden: Brill, 2001.

Cohen, H. Floris. "Review Essay." In "From West to East, from East to West? Early Science between Civilizations." *Early Science and Medicine* 17 (2012): 339–50.

Colin, Auguste. "Lettres sur l'Égypte: Industries manufacturières." *Revue des Deux Mondes* 14, no. 4 (1838): 517–31.

Conermann, Stephan, and Tilman Seindensticker. "Some Remarks on Ibn al-Tawq's (d. 905/1509) Journal, *al-Ta'liq*, Vol. 1 (885/1480–890/1485)." *Mamluk Studies Review* 11, no. 2 (2007): 121–35.

Connor, Clifford D. *A People's History of Science: Miners, Midwives and "Low Mechanicks."* New York: Nation Books, 2005.

Coulson, Noel. "Muslim Custom and Case Law." *Die Welt des Islam*, n.s. 6, 1, no. 2 (1959): 13–24.

Crouzet, François. "France." In *The Industrial Revolution in National Context: Europe and the USA*, edited by Mukilas Teich and Roy Porter, 36–63. Cambridge: Cambridge University Press, 1996.

Crozet, Pascal. *Les Sciences modernes en Égypte, transfert et appropriation, 1805–1902*. Paris: Guethner, 2008.

Cuno, Kenneth M. "Ideology and Juridical Discourse in Ottoman Egypt: The Use of the Concept of *Irsad*." *Islamic Law and Society* 6, no. 2 (1999): 136–63.

al-Damurdashi. *Al-Damurdashi's Chronicle of Egypt, 1688–1755, al-Durra al-Musana fi Akhbar al-Kinana*, translated and annotated by Daniel Crecelius and Abd al-Wahhab Bakr. Leiden: Brill, 1991.

Dana, Jean-Pierre-Marie. "Observations sur la préparation du carthame, ou safron bâtard, nommé le *linnée carthamus tinctirius*." In *Mémoire de l'Académie de Science à Turin, Année 1792 à 1800*. Vol. 6. Turin: Imprimerie Nationale, 1801.

Davies, Humphrey, ed. *Yusuf al-Shirbini's* Kitab Hazz al-Quhuf bi-Sharh Qasid Abi Shaduf *(Brains Confounded by the Ode of Abu Shaduf Expounded)*. Vol. 1. Leuven: Peeters, 2005.

Dayf, Shawqi. *Tahrifat al-'amiya li-l-fusha*. Cairo: Dar al-Ma'arif, 1994.

Delametherie, J.-Cl. *Journal de physique, de chimie, d'histoire naturelle et des arts*. Vol. 51. Paris: Chez Fuchs, 1800.

Denon, Vivant. *Voyage dans la basse et haute Égypte pendant les campagnes du général Bonaparte*. Paris: Imprimerie Didot l'Aîné, An X/1802.

Descotils et Berthollet. "Observations sur les qualités tinctoriales du henneh." In *La Décade Égyptienne*. Vol. 2. An VIII/1800.

Diem, Werner. *Arabische amtliche Briefe des 10. bis 16. Jahrhunderts aus der Österreichischen Nationalbibliothek in Wien*. Wiesbaden: Harrassowitz, 1996.

———. *Arabische Privatbriefe des 9. bis 15. Jahrhunderts aus der Österreichischen Nationalbibliothek in Wien*. Wiesbaden: Harrassowitz, 1996.

Doss, Madiha. "Military Chronicles of 17th-century Egypt as an Aspect of Popular Culture." In *Proceedings of the Colloquium on Logos, Ethos, Mythos in the Middle East and North Africa*, edited by K. Devenyi and T. Ivanyi, 67–79. Budapest: Eötvös Loránd University Chair for Arabic Studies and Csoma de Kőrős Society, Section of Islamic Studies, 1996.

———. "Réflections sur le début de l'écriture dialectique en Égypte." *Égypte/Monde Arabe* 27–28 (1996): 119–46.

———. "Some Remarks on the Oral Factor in Arabic Linguistics." In *Dialectica Arabica: A Collection of Articles in Honour of the Sixtieth Birthday of Professor Heikki Palva*, 49–61. Helsinki: Finnish Oriental Society, 1995.

Doss, Madiha, and Humphrey Davies, eds. *al-'Amiya al-misriya al-maktuba*. Cairo: al-Hay'a al-Misriya al-Amma li-l-Kitab, 2013.

Dumas, Jean-Baptiste. *Précis de l'art de la teinture*. Paris: Bechet Jeune, 1846.

———. *Traité de chimie appliquée aux arts*. Vol. 8. Paris: Imprimerie Alexandre Bailly, 1846.

DuPlessis, Robert. "Cotton Consumption in the Seventeenth and Eighteenth Century North Atlantic." In *The Spinning World: A Global History of Cotton Textiles, 1200–1850*, edited by Giorgio Riello and Prasannan Parthasarathi, 227–60. Oxford: Oxford University Press, 2009.

Eldem, Edhem. "French Trade and Commercial Policy in the Levant in the Eighteenth Century." *Oriente Moderne Nuova Serie* 18, no. 79 (1999): 27–47.

Establet, Colette, and Jean-Paul Pascual. "Les tissus dans les boutiques, les tissus dans les maisons: Damas vers 1700." *Rives nord-méditerrannéenes* 29 (2008): 107–24.

———. *Des tissus et des hommes: Damas vers 1700*. Damascus: Institut français du Proche-Orient, 2005.

Fahmy, Ziad. *Ordinary Egyptians: Creating the Modern Nation through Popular Culture*. Palo Alto, CA: Stanford University Press, 2011.

Fairlie, Susan. "Dyestuffs in the Eighteenth Century." *Economic History Review*, n.s., 17, no. 3 (1965): 488–510.

Faroqhi, Suraiya. *Artisans and Empire: Crafts and Craftspeople under the Ottomans*. London: I.B.Tauris, 2011.

———. "Declines and Revivals in Textile Production." In *Cambridge History of Turkey: The Later Ottoman Empire, 1603–1839*, edited by Suraiya Faroqhi. Vol. 3, 356–75. Cambridge: Cambridge University Press, 2006.

———. "Immigrant Tradesmen as Guild Members, or the Adventures of Tunisian Fez-sellers in Eighteenth-century Istanbul." In *The Arab Lands in the Ottoman Era (1600–1900): In Honor of Caesar Farah*, edited by Jane Hathaway, 187–207. Minneapolis: Center of Early Modern History, 2009.

———. "Ottoman Cotton Textiles, 1500s to 1800: The Story of a Success That Did Not Last." In *The Spinning World: A Global History of Cotton Textiles, 1200–1850*, edited by Giorgio Riello and Prasannan Parthasarathi, 89–104. Oxford: Oxford University Press, 2009.

———. *The Ottoman Empire and the World around It*. London: I.B.Tauris, 2004.

Figuier, Louis. *Les Merveilles de l'Industrie*. Paris: Furne, Jouvet et Cie, 1860.

Flachat, Jean-Claude. *Observations sur le commerce et sur les arts*. Lyon: Chez Jacquenod père et Rusand, 1766.

Flachat, Stéphane. *L'industrie: Recueil des traités élémentaires sur l'industrie française et étrangère*. Paris: Tenre et Dupuy, imprimeurs-éditeurs, 1834.

Fletcher, Joseph. "Integrative History: Parallels and Interconnections in the Early Modern Period, 1500–1800." *Journal of Turkish Studies* 9 (1985): 37–57.

Frank, André Gunder. *ReOrient: Global Economy in the Asian Age*. Berkeley: University of California Press, 1998.

Franz-Murphy, Gladys. "Arabic Papyrology and Middle Eastern Studies." *Middle East Studies Association Bulletin* 19, no. 1 (July 1985): 34–48.

———. "A Comparison of the Arabic and Earlier Egyptian Contract Formularies, Part I: The Arabic Contracts from Egypt, 3rd/9th–5th /11th Centuries." *Journal of Near-East Studies* 40, no. 3 (July 1981): 203–25.

Furnari, Salvatore. *Traité pratique des maladies des yeux*. Paris: Chez J.-B. Baillière, 1841.

Gekas, Athanasios. "A Global History of Ottoman Cotton Textiles, 1600–1850." *EUI Working Papers*, No. 2007/30, European University Institute, 1–23. San Domenico di Fiesola, Italy: Badia Fiesolana, 2007.

Geoffroy, Eric. "La 'seconde vague': fin XIIIe siècle–XV siècle." In *Les Voies d'Allah, les orders mystiques dans le monde musulman des origins à aujourd'hui*, edited by Alexandre Popovic and Gilles Veinstein, 55–67. Paris: Fayard, 1996.

———. *Le soufisme en Égypte et en Syrie*. Damascus: Institut français de Damas, 1996.

Gerber, Haim. *Islamic Law and Culture 1600–1840*. Leiden: Brill, 1999.

Gervase Clarence-Smith, William. "Technological and Scientific Change in Early Modern Islam, 1450–1850." Paper given at the XIV International Economic History Congress, Helsinki, 2006.

Gillow, John. *Textiles of the Islamic World*. London: Thames and Hudson, 2010.

Girard, Pierre-Simon. "Mémoire sur l'agriculture, l'industrie et le commerce de l'Égypte." In *Description de l'Égypte, État Moderne*. Vol. 2, no. 1, 1–259. Paris: Panckoucke 1812; repub. as independent booklet: Paris: Imprimerie Royale, 1822.

Goffman, Daniel. *The Ottoman Empire and Early Modern Europe*. Cambridge: Cambridge University Press, 2002.

Goody, Jack. *The Theft of History*. Cambridge: Cambridge University Press, 2008.

Gran, Peter. *Beyond Eurocentrism: A New View of World History*. Syracuse, NY: Syracuse University Press, 1996.

———. *Islamic Roots of Capitalism: Egypt 1760–1840*. Cairo: American University in Cairo Press, 1999.

Granger, M. *Relation du Voyage en Égypte par le Sieur Granger fait en 1730*. Paris: Chez Jacques Vincent, 1745.

Grehan, James. "The Mysterious Power of Words: Language, Law and Culture in Ottoman Damascus (17th–18th Centuries)." *Journal of Social History* (Summer 2004): 991–1015.

Grob, Eva Maria. *Documentary Arabic Private and Business Letters on Papyrus*. Berlin: de Gruyter, 2010.

Gully, Adrian. "Epistles or Grammarians: Illustrations from the *insha* Literature." *British Journal of Middle East Studies* 23, no. 2 (Nov. 1996): 147–66.

Guo, Li. "Paradise Lost: Ibn Daniyal's Response to Baybar's Campaign against Vice in Cairo." *Journal of the American Oriental Society* 121, no. 2 (April–June 2001): 219–35.

Hallaq, Wael. "A Prelude to Ottoman Reform: Ibn Abidin on Custom and Legal Change." In *Histories of the Modern Middle East: New Directions*, edited by Israel Gershoni, Y. Hakam Erdem, and Ursula Wokock, 37–62. Boulder, CO: Lynne Rienner, 2002.

Hanna, Nelly. *Artisan Entrepreneurs in Cairo and Early Modern Capitalism (1600–1800)*. Syracuse, NY: Syracuse University Press, 2011.

———. "The Chronicles of Ottoman Egypt: History or Entertainment?" In *The Historiography of Islamic Egypt (c. 950–1800)*, edited by Hugh Kennedy, 237–50. Leiden: Brill, 2001.

———. "Guild Waqf between Religious Law and Common Law." In *Held in Trust*, edited by Pascale Ghazaleh, 165–89. Cairo: American University in Cairo Press, 2011.

———. "History from Below, Dictionary from Below." In *Innovations in Islam: Traditions and Contributions*, edited by Mehran Kamrava, 85–97. Los Angeles: University of California Press, 2011.

———. *In Praise of Books: A Cultural History of Cairo's Middle Class, 16th–18th Centuries*. Syracuse, NY: Syracuse University Press, 2003.

———. "Self Narratives in Arabic Texts 1500–1800." In *The Uses of First Person Writings: Africa, America, Asia, Europe*, edited by François-Joseph Ruggio, 139–54. Brussels: Peter Lang, 2013.

Hasselquist, Frederic. *Voyage dans le Levant dans les années 1749, 1750, 1751, et 1752*. Paris: Chez Saugrain le jeune, 1769.

Hilaire-Pérez, Liliane. "Cultures pratiques et techniques de l'échange entre Lyon et le Levant: inventions et réseaux au XVIIIe siècle." *Revue d'histoire moderne et contemporaine* 49, no. 1 (2002): 89–114.

———. "Transferts technologiques, droit et territoires: le cas franco-anglais au XVIIIe siècle." *Revue d'histoire moderne et contemporaine* 44, no. 4 (Oct.–Dec. 1997): 547–79.

Holt, Peter. "The Career of Kucuk Muhammad (1676–1694)." *Bulletin of the School of Oriental and African Studies* 26, no. 2 (1963): 269–87.

———. "Ottoman Egypt (1517–1798): An Account of Arabic Historical Sources." In *Political and Social Change in Modern Egypt*, edited by P.M. Holt, 3–12. London: Oxford University Press, 1968.

Huff, Toby E. *Intellectual Curiosity and the Scientific Revolution: A Global Perspective*. Cambridge: Cambridge University Press, 2011.

———. *The Rise of Early Modern Science: Islam, China, and the West*. 2nd ed. Cambridge: Cambridge University Press, 1993, 2003.

Humbert, Jean-Marcel. *Égyptomanie: la passion de l'Égypte*. Paris: Les Musées de la ville de Paris, 2000.

———. *L'Égyptomanie: sources, thèmes et symboles, étude de la réutilisation des thèmes décoratifs empruntés à l'Égypte ancienne*. Paris: ANRT, 1990.

Hunt, Janin. *The Pursuit of Learning in the Islamic World, 610–2003*. Jefferson, NC: McFarland, 2005.

Ibn Abidin. N.d. *Majmu'at rasa'il Ibn Abidin*. Beirut: Ihya al-Turath al-Arabi.

Ibn al-Tawq, Shihab al-Din Ahmad. *Al-Ta'liq, Yawmiyat Shihab al-Din Ahmad Ibn al-Tawq*, edited by Shaykh Jaafar al-Muhajir. 3 vols. Damascus: IFEAD, 2000–2004.

Ibn Hanbali, Radiy al-Din Yusuf. *Bahr al-awam fi-ma asab fihi al-awwam*, edited by Sha'ban Salih. Cairo: Dar al-Thaqafa al-Arabiya, 1990.

Ibn Kannan al-Salihi, Muhammad. *Yawmiyat shamiya*, edited by Akram Hasan al-'Ulabi. Damascus: Dar al-Tabba', n.d.

Ibn Khaldun. *al-Muqaddima*. Beirut: Dar al-Awda, 1981.

Ibn Nujaym. *al-Ashbah wa-l-natha'ir 'ala madhhab Abi Hanifa al-Nu'man*. Beirut: Dar al-Kutub al-Ilmiya, 1985.

Ibn Sudun. *Bringing a Laugh to a Scowling Face: A Study and Critical Edition of the* Nuzhat al-nufus wa-mudhik al-a'bus, edited by Arnoud Vrolijk. Leiden: School of Asian, African and Amerindian Studies, 1998.

Ilardi, Vincent. *Renaissance Vision from Spectacles to Telescopes*. Philadelphia: American Philosophical Society, 2007.

Inalcik, Halil. "Capital in the Ottoman Empire." *The Journal of Economic History* 29, no. 1 (March 1969): 97–140.

———. *An Economic and Social History of the Ottoman Empire*. Vol. 1, *1300–1600*. Cambridge: Cambridge University Press, 1994.

———. "Kutn: In the Ottoman Empire." In *Encyclopedia of Islam*. Vol. 5. 2nd ed. Edited by P. Bearman et al., 557–66. Leiden: Brill, 1982.

al-Jabarti. *Abd al-Rahman al-Jabarti's History of Egypt*, Ajaib al-Athar fi'l Tarajim wa'l-Akhbar, edited by Thomas Philipp and Moshe Perlmann, vol. 1, 664–65. Stuttgart: Franz Steiner Verlag, 1994.

———. *'Aja'ib al-athar fi-l-tarajim wa-l-akhbar.* Vol. 1. Edited by Abdul-Rahim Abdul-Rahman Abdul-Rahim. Cairo: Dar al-Kutub al-Misriya, 1998.

Jaubert, Pierre. *Dictionnaire raisonné universel des arts et des métiers*. Vol. 4. Lyon: Chez Amable Leroy, 1801.

Johansen, Baber. *The Islamic Law on Land Tax and Rent*. London: Croom Helm, 1988.

Johnson, Gordon, David Arnold, C.A. Bayly, John F. Richards, Stewart Gordon, Om Prakash, Susan Bayly, and David Ludden. "Introduction: Science, Colonialism, and Modernity." In *The New Cambridge History of India, Science, Technology, and Medicine in Colonial India.* Vols. 3–5. Edited by Gordon Johnson et al. 1–8. Cambridge: Cambridge University Press, 2000.

Jomard, Edmé François. "Description de la ville et de la citadelle du Kaire." In *Description de l'Égypte, état moderne*, vol. 1, 113–509. Paris: Imprimerie Panckoucke, 1829.

Katsiardi-Hering, Olga. "The Allure of Red Cotton Yarn and How It Came to Vienna: Associations of Greek Artisans and Merchants Operating between the Ottoman and the Hapsburg Empires." In *Merchants in the Ottoman Empire*, edited by Suraiya Faroqhi and Gilles Veinstein, 97–131. Paris and Louvain: Peeters, 2008.

Kelly, Catherine. "Medicine and the Egyptian Campaign: The Development of the Military Medical Officer during the Napoleonic Wars c. 1798–1801." *Canadian Bulletin of Medical History* 27, no. 2 (2010): 321–42.

Keyder, Caglar. "Creation and Destruction of Forms of Manufacturing: The Ottoman Example." In *Between Development and Underdevelopment, 1800–1870*, edited by Jean Batou, 157–79. Geneva: Center for International Economic History, 1991.

al-Khafaji, Shihab al-Din Ahmad. *Shifa al-ghalil fima fi kalam al-'Arab min al-dakhil*, edited by Muhamad Abdul Munim Khafaji. Cairo: al-Maktaba al-Azhariya li-l-Turath, 2003.

Khalidi, Tarif. *Arab Historical Thought in the Classical Period*. Cambridge: Cambridge University Press, 1996.

Khalil, Sahar Ali Hanafi Ali. "Al-'Ilaqat al tugariya bayn Misr wa Bilad al-Sham al-Kubra fi-l-qarn al-thamin 'ashar." PhD diss., Cairo University, Faculty of Arts, 1998.

Kucukkalay, A. Mesud. "Imports to Smyrna from 1792 to 1804: New Statistics from the Ottoman Sources." *Journal of the Economic and Social History of the Orient* 51, no. 3 (2008): 487–512.

Kucukkalay, A. Mesud, and Numan Elibol. "Ottoman Imports in the Eighteenth Century: Smyrna (1771–72)." *Middle Eastern Studies* 42, no. 5 (Sept. 2006): 723–40.

Kuran, Timur. *The Great Divergence: How Islamic Law Held Back the Middle East*. Princeton, NJ: Princeton University Press, 2011.

———. "Islam and Underdevelopment: An Old Puzzle Revisited." *Journal of Institutional and Theoretical Economics* 151, no. 1 (March 1997): 41–71.

Labouchere, Alfred. *Oberkampf, 1738–1815*. Paris: Librairie Hachette, 1866.

Landes, David. *Prometheus Unbound: Technological Change and Industrial Development in Western Europe from 1750 to the Present*. Cambridge: Cambridge University Press, 2003.

———. *The Unbound Prometheus: Technological Change and Industrial Development in Western Europe from 1750 to the Present*. Cambridge: Cambridge University Press, 1969.

Larkin, Margaret. "Popular Poetry in the Post-Classical Period." In *The Cambridge History of Arabic Literature*. Vol. 6. *Arabic Literature in the Post-Classical Period*, edited by Roger Allen and D.S. Richards, 191–210. Cambridge: Cambridge University Press, 2006.

Lehning, James. *Peasant and French: Cultural Contact in Rural France during the Nineteenth Century*. Cambridge: Cambridge University Press, 1995.

Lellouch, Benjamin. "Le téléphone arabe au Caire au lendemain de la conquête ottomane: on-dits et rumeurs dans Ibn Iyâs." *Revue du monde musulman et de la Méditerranée*, 75–76 (1995): 117–30.

Lemire, Beverly, and Giorgio Riello. "Textile and Fashion in Early Modern Europe." *Journal of Social History* 41, no. 1 (2008): 887–916.

Leuchs, Johann Carl. *Traité complet des propriétés, de la préparation et de l'emploi des matières tinctoriales et des couleurs*. Paris: Imprimerie Fournier, 1829.

Levi, Scott Cameron. *The Indian Diaspora in Central Asia and Its Trade, 1550–1900*. Leiden: Brill, 2001.

Libson, Gideon. "On the Development of Custom as a Source of Law in Islamic Law." *Islamic Law and Society* 4, no. 2 (1997): 131–55.

Little, Donald. "Mujir al-Din al-'Ulaymi's Vision of Jerusalem in the Ninth/Fifteenth Century." *Journal of the American Oriental Society* 115, no. 2 (April–July 1995): 237–47.

Lobligeois, Mireille. "Ateliers publics et filatures privées à Pondichéry après 1816." *Bulletin de l'École française d'Extrême-Orient* 59 (1972): 3–100.

Long, Pamela O. *Artisan/Practitioners and the Rise of the New Sciences, 1400–1600*. Corvallis, OR: Oregon State University Press, 2011.

Lowengard, Susan. "Colours and Colour-Making in the Eighteenth Century." In *Consumers and Luxury: Consumer Culture in Europe, 1650–1850*, edited by Maxine Berg and Helen Clifford, 103–18. Manchester: Manchester University Press, 1999.

———. *The Creation of Colour in Eighteenth-century Europe*. New York: Columbia University Press, 2006.

Mackie, Louise. "Towards an Understanding of Mamluk Silks: National and International Connections." *Muqarnas* 2 (1984): 127–46.

Macquer, Pierre-Joseph. *Dictionnaire de Chimie contenant la Théorie et la Pratique de cette science*. Vol. 1. Paris: Imprimerie de Monsieur, 1778.

de Maillet, Benoît. *Description de l'Égypte . . . composé sur les mémoires de M. de Maillet, ancien consul de France au Caire, par M. l'Abbé Le Mascrier.* Paris: Chez Louis Genneau et Jacques Rollin, 1735.

Makki, Muhammad b. Muhammad. *Tarikh Makka al-Musharaffa*. Beirut: Dar al-Kutub al-Ilmiya, 1997.

Mandaville, Jon. "The Ottoman Court Records of Syria and Jordan." *Journal of the American Oriental Society* 86, no. 3 (July–Sept. 1966): 311–19.

———. "Usurious Piety: The Cash Waqf Controversy in the Ottoman Empire." *International Journal of Middle East Studies* 10, no. 3 (Aug. 1979): 289–308.

Mann, Michael. "'Torch Bearers Upon the Path of Progress,' Britain's Ideology of a Moral and Material Progress in India: An Introductory Essay." In *Colonialism as a Civilizing Mission: Cultural Ideology in British*

India, edited by Harald Fischer-Tine and Michael Mann, 4–10. London: Anthem Press, 2004.

Marzuq, Khaled Sayid, ed. *Min watha'iq Bani Suwayf fi-l-'asr al-'uthmani, sijjil min mahkama Bab al-Ali*. Cairo: Dar al-Kutub wa-l-Watha'iq, 2012.

Maskiell, Michelle. "Consuming Kashmir: Shawls and Empire, 1500–2000." *Journal of World History* 13, no. 1 (Spring 2002): 27–65.

Masters, Bruce. "The View from the Province: Syrian Chronicles of the Eighteenth Century." *Journal of the American Oriental Society* 114, no. 3 (July–Sept. 1994): 353–62.

Mayeur-Jouen, Catherine, and Nicolas Michel. "Cheikhs, *zawiyas* et confréries du Delta central: un paysage religieux autour du XVIe siècle." In *Sociétés rurales ottomanes*, edited by Muhammad Afifi, Rachida Chih, Brigitte Marino, Nicolas Michel, and Isik Tamdogan, 139–62. Cairo: IFAO, 2005.

"Mémoire sur l'ophthalmie endémique en Égypte." In *Description de l'Égypte*. Vol. 13. *État Moderne*. 2nd ed., 36–50. Paris: Panckoucke, 1823.

Michel, Nicolas. "Langues et écritures des papiers publics dans l'Égypte ottoman." *Égypte/Monde Arabe* 27–28 (1996): 157–84.

Milad, Salwa Ali. *al-Watha'iq al-'uthmaniya: dirasa arshifiya watha'iqiya li-sijillat mahkama al-Bab al-Ali*. Alexandria: Dar al-Thaqafa al-'Ilmiya, 2000.

Mitchell, Timothy. "The State of Modernity." In *Questions of Modernity*, edited by Timothy Mitchell, 2–3. Toronto: University of Toronto Press, 1994.

Moreh, Shmuel. *Studies in Modern Arabic Prose and Poetry*. Leiden: Brill, 1987.

Morray, David. *An Ayyubid Notable and His World: Ibn al-Adim and Aleppo as Portrayed in His Biographical Dictionary of People Associated with the City*. Leiden: Brill, 1994.

Mortel, Richard. "The Decline of Mamluk Civil Bureaucracy in the Fifteenth Century: The Career of Abul-Khayr al-Nahhas." *Journal of Islamic Studies* 6, no. 2 (1995): 173–88.

Mugglestone, Lynda. "The Rise of Received Pronunciation." In *A Companion to the History of the English Language*, edited by Haruko Momma and Michael Matto, 243–50. Chichister: Blackwell, 2008.

al-Muhibbi, Muhammad Amin. *Qasd al-sabil fima fi-l-lugha al-'arabiya min al-dakhil*. 2 vols. Edited by 'Uthman Mahmud al-Sini. Riyadh: Maktabat al-Tawba, 1994.

Mungello, D.E. *The Great Encounter of China and the West 1500–1800*. Lanham, MD: Rowman and Littlefield, 2013.

Nicholson, William, ed. *Journal of Natural Philosophy, Chemistry and the Arts.* Vol. 4. Printed for the author by London: Stratford, Crowncourt, and Temple Bar, 1801.

Nieto-Galan, Agusti. "Between Craft Routines and Academic Rules: Natural Dyestuffs and the 'Art' of Dyeing in the Eighteenth Century." In *Materials and Expertise in Early Modern Europe: Between Market and Laboratory*, edited by Ursula Klein and E.C. Spary, 321–53. Chicago: University of Chicago Press, 2010.

O'Reilly, R. *Essai sur le blanchiment, avec la description de la nouvelle méthode.* Paris: Chez Deterville, An IX/1801.

Owen, Roger. *Cotton and the Egyptian Economy, 1820–1914: A Study in Trade and Development.* Oxford: Clarendon, 1969.

Palva, Heikki. "Linguistic Notes on a Dialectical 17th–18th Century Egyptian Arabic Narrative." *Oriente Moderne*, n.s. 80 (2000): 83–97.

Pamuk, Sevket. "Institutional Change and the Longevity of the Ottoman Empire, 1500–1800." *Journal of Interdisciplinary History* 35, no. 2 (Autumn 2004): 225–47.

———. *A Monetary History of the Ottoman Empire*. Cambridge: Cambridge University Press, 2000.

Pamuk, Sevket, and Jeffrey Williamson. "Ottoman De-industrialization 1800–1913: Assessing the Magnitude, Impact and Response." *The Economic History Review* 64, S1 (Feb. 2011): 159–84.

Parker, Charles. *Global Interactions in the Early Modern Age, 1400–1800.* Cambridge: Cambridge University Press, 2010.

Parthasarathi, Prasannan. *The Transition to a Colonial Economy: Weavers, Merchants, and Kings in South India, 1720–1800.* Cambridge: Cambridge University Press, 2001.

———. *Why Europe Grew Rich and Asia Did Not: Global Economic Divergence, 1600–1850.* New York: Cambridge University Press, 2011.

Parthasarathi, Prasannan, and Giorgio Riello. "Introduction: Cotton Textiles and Global History." In *The Spinning World: A Global History of Cotton Textiles, 1200–1850*, edited by Giorgio Riello and Prasannan Parthasarathi, 1–13. Oxford: Oxford University Press, 2009.

Peled, M. "Nodding the Necks: A Literary Study of Shirbini's "Hazz al-Quhuf." *Die Welt des Islam*, n.s. 26, nos. 1–4 (1986): 57–75.

Peltier, Jean-Gabriel. *Paris pendant l'année 1800.* Vol. 28. London: Imprimerie T. Baylis, 1800.

Perlin, Frank. "Monetary Revolution and Societal Change in the Late Medieval and Early Modern Times: A Review Article." *The Journal of Asian Studies* 45, no. 5 (Nov. 1986): 1037–49.

Petry, Carl. *Protectors or Praetorians: The Last Mamluk Sultans and Egypt's Waning as a Great Power*. Albany, NY: State University of New York Press, 1994.

Peuchet, Jacques. *Bibliothèque commercial*. Vol. 2. Paris: Chez Buisson, 1803.

———. *Dictionnaire universel de la géographie commerçante*. Vol. 5. Paris: Chez Blanchon, An VIII/1800.

Piesse, Louis. *Itinéraire historique et descriptif de l'Algérie, comprenant le Tell et le Sahara*. Paris: Imprimerie de Ch. Lahure, 1862.

Le Pileur d'Apligny. *L'art de la teinture des fils et des étoffes de coton précédés d'une théorie*. Paris: Chez Moutard, Libraire de la Reine, Quai des Augustins, 1776.

Pireto, Andrés I. *Missionary Scientists: Jesuit Science in Spanish South America, 1570–1810*. Nashville, TN: Vanderbilt University Press, 2011.

de la Platière, Jean-Marie Roland. *Encyclopédie méthodique: Manufactures, arts et métiers*. Vol. 1. Paris: Panckoucke, 1785.

Pollock, Sheldon. "Cosmopolitan and Vernacular in History." *Public Culture* 12, no. 3 (2000): 591–625.

———. "The Cosmopolitan Vernacular." *The Journal of Asian Studies* 57, no. 1 (Feb. 1998): 6–37.

———. "The Language of Science in Early Modern India." In *Forms of Knowledge in Early Modern Asia*, edited by Sheldon Pollock, 19–48. Durham, NC: Duke University Press, 2011.

Pomeranz, Kenneth. *The Great Divergence: China, Europe and the Making of the Modern World Economy*. Princeton, NJ: Princeton University Press, 2000.

Rafeq, Abdul-Karim. "Craft Organization, Work Ethics, and the Strains of Change in Ottoman Syria." *Journal of the American Oriental Society* 111, no. 3 (July–Sept. 1991): 495–511.

———. "The Economic Organization of Cities in Ottoman Syria." In *The Urban Social History of the Middle East, 1750–1950*, edited by Peter Sluglett, 104–22. Syracuse, NY: Syracuse University Press, 2008.

Raj, Kapil. "Colonial Encounters and the Forging of New Knowledge and National Identities: Great Britain and India, 1760–1850." *Osiris*, 2nd ser., 15 (2000): 119–34.

———. *Relocating Modern Science: Circulation and the Construction of Knowledge in South Asia and Europe, 1650–1900*. London: Palgrave, 2007.

Rapp, Richard. "The Unmaking of the Mediterranean Trade Hegemony: International Trade Rivalry and the Commercial Revolution." *The Journal of Economic History* 35, no. 5 (1975): 499–525.

Rashed, Roshdi. *The Development of Arabic Mathematics: Between Arithmetic and Algebra*. Dordrecht, Netherlands: Kluwer Academic Publishers, 1994.

Raveaux, Olivier. "À la façon du Levant et de Perse': Marseilles et la naissance de l'indiennage européen, 1648–1689." In *Rives nord-méditerranéennes*: "Les textiles en Méditerranée (XVe–XIXe siècle)," http://rives.revues.org/document1303.html

———. "The Birth of the Calico Printing in Europe: The Case of Marseilles (1648–1692)." Paper presented at the GEHN conference "Global Histories of Economic Development: Cotton Textiles and Other Global Industries in the Early Modern Period." Fondation Les Treilles, March 2006.

———. "Spaces and Technologies in the Cotton Industry in the Seventeenth and Eighteenth Centuries: The Example of Printed Calicoes in Marseilles." *Textile History* 36, no. 2 (Nov. 2005): 131–45.

Raymond, André. *Artisans et commerçants au Caire au XVIIIe siècle*. 2 vols. Damascus: Institut français de Damas, 1974.

———. "Une liste des corporations de métiers au Caire en 1801." *Arabica* 4, no. 2 (May 1957): 150–63.

Reichmuth, Stefan. *The World of Murtada al-Zabidi (1732–91): Life, Networks and Writing*. Oxford: Gibb Memorial Trust, 2009.

Reid, Anthony. *Southeast Asia in the Age of Commerce, 1450–1680*. Vol. 1, *The Land below the Winds*. New Haven: Yale University Press, 1993.

Richards, John F. "Early Modern India and World History." *Journal of World History* 8, no. 2 (Fall 1997): 197–209.

Riello, Giorgio. *Cotton: The Fabric That Made the Modern World*. Cambridge: Cambridge University Press, 2013.

———."The Globalization of Cotton Textiles: Indian Cottons, Europe, and the Atlantic World, 1600–1850." In *The Spinning World: A Global History of Cotton Textiles, 1200–1850*, edited by Giorgio Riello and Prasannan Parthasarathi, 261–87. Oxford: Oxford University Press, 2009.

Riello, Giorgio, and Tirthankar Roy. "Indian Textiles, Indian Ocean, and the World Economy." In *How India Clothed the World: The World of South*

Asian Textiles, 1500–1850, edited by Giorgio Riello and Tirthankar Roy, 1–30. Leiden: Brill, 2009.

Robinson, Chase. *Islamic Historiography*. Cambridge: Cambridge University Press, 2003.

Rosenthal, Franz. *History of Muslim Historiography*. Leiden: Brill, 1968.

Roubaud, Pierre-Joseph-André. *Histoire générale de l'Afrique, de l'Asie et de l'Amérique*. Vol. 9. Paris: Chez des Ventes de la Doue, 1771.

Sajdi, Dana. "A Room of His Own: The 'History' of the Barber of Damascus (fl. 1762)." *MIT Electronic Journal of Middle East Studies* 3 (Fall 2003): 19–35.

Saliba, George. *Islamic Science and the Making of the Renaissance*. Cambridge, MA: MIT Press, 2007.

Salih, Ahmad Rushdi. *al-Adab al-sha'bi*. 3rd ed. Cairo: Maktabat al-Nahda al-Misriya, 1971.

Savage-Smith, Emilie. "Islam." In *The Cambridge History of Science*, Vol. 4, *Eighteenth-Century Science*, edited by Roy Porter, 648–86. Cambridge: Cambridge University Press, 2003.

Scheffer, M. *Essai sur l'art de la teinture*. Paris: Chez Goeury, 1803.

Secord, James A. "Knowledge in Transit," *Isis* 95, no. 4 (Dec. 2004): 654–72.

Singh, Nagendra Kr., and A. Samiuddin, eds. *Encyclopedic Historiography of the Muslim World*. Vol. 1. Delhi: Global Vision, 2003.

Smith, Pamela. *The Body of the Artisan: Art and Experience in the Scientific Revolution*. Chicago: University of Chicago Press, 2004.

Sonnini, Charles Sigisbert. *Voyage dans la Haute et Basse Égypte*. Vol. 1. Paris: F. Buisson, An VII/1799.

Soravia, Bruna. "Les manuels à l'usage des fonctionnaires de l'administration ("Adab al-Katib") dans l'Islam classique." *Arabica* 52, no. 3 (July 2005): 417–36.

Stern, Steve. "Feudalism, Capitalism and World System in the Perspective of Latin America and the Caribbean." *American Historical Review* 94, no. 4 (Oct. 1988): 829–72.

al-Suyuti, Jalal al-Din. *Husn al-muhadara fi tarikh Misr wa-l-Qahira*. Beirut: Dar al-Kutub al-Ilmiya, 1997.

Thackeray, Frank W., and John E. Findling, eds. *Events that Formed the Modern World*, Vol. 1, *From the European Renaissance through the Sixteenth Century*. Santa Barbara, CA: ABC-CLIO, 2012.

de Thevenot, Jean. *Suite du Voyage de M. de Thevenot au Levant*. Paris: Chez Charles Angot, 1689.

Thompson, E.P. *The Making of the English Working Class.* New York: Pantheon Books, 1964.

Thompson, Jon. "Late Mamluk Carpets: Some New Observations." In *The Art of the Mamluks in Egypt and Syria: Evolution and Impact*, edited by Doris Behrens-Abouseif, 115–41. Bonn: Bonn University Press, 2012.

Tresse, René. "Le Conservatoire des Arts et Métiers et la Société d'encouragement de l'industrie nationale au debut du XIX siècle." In *Revue d'histoire des sciences et de leurs applications* 5, nos. 5, 3 (1952): 246–64.

Tucker, Judith. *In the House of the Law: Gender and Islamic Law in Ottoman Syria and Palestine.* Berkeley: University of California Press, 1998.

Uthman, Naser. "La production textile à Rosette au XVIIIe siècle." *Rives Méditerranéennes* 29 (2008): 2–11.

Van Berkel, Maaike. "A Well-mannered Man of Letters or a Cunning Accountant: Qalqashandi and the Historical Position of the *katib*." *Masaq: Islam and the Medieval Mediterranean* 13 (2001): 87–95.

Vansleb, F. *The Present State of Egypt or a New Relation of a Late Voyage into that Kingdom Performed in the Years 1672 and 1673.* London: R.E. John Starkey, 1678. Repr. Westmead: Gregg International, 1972.

Van Steenbergen, Jo. "Qalawunid Discourse, Elite Communication and the Mamluk Cultural Matrix: Interpreting a 14th-century Panegyric." *Journal of Arabic Literature* 43, no. 1 (2012): 1–28.

Veinstein, Gilles. "Commercial Relations between India and the Ottoman Empire (Late Fifteenth to Late Eighteenth Century): A Few Notes and Hypothesis." In *Merchants, Companies, and Trade: Europe and Asia in the Early Modern Era*, edited by Suchil Chaudhury and Michel Morineau, 95–115. Cambridge: Cambridge University Press, 1999.

Vitalis, J.B. *Manuel du Teinturier sur filé et sur coton filé.* Rouen: Chez Megard, 1810.

Volney, Constantin-François. *Les oeuvres complètes de Volney.* Paris: Didot, 1838.

———. *Travels through Syria and Egypt in the Years 1783, 1784, and 1785.* 2 vols. Repub. Westmead: Gregg International, 1972.

———. *Voyage en Égypte et en Syrie pendant les années 1783, 1784, et 1785.* Vol. 2. Paris: Parmantier, 1825.

de Vries, Jan. "The Industrial Revolution and the Industrious Revolution." *The Journal of Economic History* 54, no. 2 (June 1994): 249–70.

Walker, Bethany J. "Rethinking Mamluk Textiles." *Mamluk Studies Review* 4 (2000): 167–217.

Wallerstein, Immanuel. *The Modern World System.* Berkeley: University of California Press, 2011.

Wansbrough, John. "A Mamluk Letter of 877/1473." *Bulletin of the School of Oriental and African Studies* 24, no. 2 (1961): 200–13.

Washbrook, David. "From Comparative Sociology to Global History: Britain and India in the Pre-history of Modernity." *Journal of the Economic and Social History of the Orient* 40, no. 4 (1997): 410–43.

———. "A Global History of Modernity: A Response to a Reply." *Journal of the Economic and Social History of the Orient* 41, no. 3 (1998): 295–311.

———. "Merchants, Markets and Commerce in Early Modern Southern India." *Journal of the Economic and Social History of the Orient* 53 (2010): 266–89.

Williams, Eric. *Capitalism and Slavery*. Chapel Hill, NC: University of North Carolina Press, 1944.

Willis, John E. "European Consumption and Asian Production in the Seventeenth and Eighteenth Century." In *Consumption and the World of Goods*, edited by John Brewer and Roy Porter, 133–57. London: Routledge, 1993.

Wolf, Eric. *Europe and the People without History*. Berkeley: University of California Press, 2010.

Woodhead, Christine. "Reading Ottoman Sehnames: Official Historiography in the Late Sixteenth Century." *Studia Islamica* 104–105 (2007): 67–80.

Yi, Eungeong. *Guild Dynamics in Seventeenth-century Istanbul: Fluidity and Leverage*. Leiden: Brill, 2004.

Yildirim, Onur. "Transformation of the Craft Guilds in Istanbul (1650–1850)." *Islamic Studies* 40, no. 1 (Spring 2001): 49–66.

Yusoff, Kamaruzaman. "An Overview of the Ms., 'The Paris Fragment,' on the History of Ottoman Egypt in the Seventeenth Century." *Islamic Quarterly* 48, no. 3 (2004): 222–37.

———. "An Overview of the Ms. 'Zubdat ikhtisar tarikh muluk Misr al-mahrusa.'" *Islamic Studies* 41, no. 2 (Summer 2002): 319–33.

Zack, Elisabeth. "Colloquial Arabic in the Seventeenth Century: Yusuf al-Magribi's Egyptian Arabic Word-List." In *Approaches to Arabic Dialects*, edited by Martine Haak, Rudolf de Jong, and Kees Versteegh, 373–90. Leiden: Brill, 2004.

Zarinebaf, Fariba. "Ottoman Guilds and the State in Eighteenth-century Istanbul." Paper presented at the conference "The Rise and Decline of Imperial Leadership." Evanston, IL: Northwestern University, November 2007.

Zubaida, Sami. *Law and Power in the Islamic World*. London: I.B.Tauris, 2003.

Index